P9-ARA-060

Sinan

MAKERS OF ISLAMIC CIVILIZATION

This series, conceived by the Oxford Centre for Islamic Studies and jointly published by Oxford University Press and I.B.Tauris, provides an introduction to outstanding figures in the history of Islamic civilization. Written by leading scholars, these books are designed to be the essential first point of reference for any reader interested in the growth and development of Islamic history and culture.

General Editor: F. A. Nizami
Series Manager: R. M. Ritter

Sinan

J. M. Rogers

Oxford Centre for Islamic Studies

I.B. TAURIS

LONDON · NEW YORK

Published in 2006 by I.B.Tauris & Co. Ltd. and Oxford University Press India
in association with the Oxford Centre for Islamic Studies

I.B.Tauris & Co. Ltd.
6 Salem Road, London W2 4BU
175 Fifth Avenue, New York NY 10010
www.ibtauris.com

In the United States of America and Canada distributed by
Palgrave Macmillan, a division of St. Martin's Press
175 Fifth Avenue, New York NY 10010

Copyright © 2006 Oxford Centre for Islamic Studies

The right of J. M. Rogers to be identified as Author of this work
has been asserted by the Licensor in accordance with the Copyright,
Designs and Patents Act 1988.

All rights reserved. Except for brief quotations in a review, this book,
or any part thereof, may not be reproduced, stored in or introduced into a
retrieval system, or transmitted, in any form or by any means, electronic,
mechanical, photocopying, recording or otherwise, without the prior written
permission of the publisher.

ISBN 1 84511 096 X
EAN 978 1 84511 096 3

For all territories except South Asia

A full CIP record for this book is available from the British Library
A full CIP record is available from the Library of Congress

Library of Congress Catalog Card Number: available

Typeset in GoudyOlst BT
by Eleven Arts, Keshav Puram, Delhi 110 035
Printed in India by De-Unique, New Delhi 110 018

Contents

Illustrations

Preface

In Islam the foundation and construction of institutions of public welfare, from mosques to water supplies, were as much the responsibility of the ruler, or his delegated agents, as of private individuals. Indeed, Muslim political theorists have traditionally held up the creation of pious foundations as one of the defining characteristics of the just ruler. The Sultan's role in patronage, both directly and indirectly, was thus paramount. Typically Islamic is the general absence of any clear distinction between the secular and the religious, for even fortresses and bridges, because of the part they played in defence against the enemies of Islam, were a pious duty; while caravansarays conduced to the prosperity of the state, and commerce made it healthy and economically viable. Moreover, those on major campaign routes could be used as barracks as and when necessary.

The upkeep of these foundations was assured by endowments (*vakf*, plural *evkâf*), which in theory were in perpetuity. They are common to all Islamic cultures, but in Ottoman Turkey while their organization owed something to the example of the Christian *piae causae* as established by the Byzantine Emperor Justinian, the role of the central power was paramount. This was not least because in the eyes of the authorities the land belonged to the Sultan, so that freehold land, an essential prerequisite of the endowment of a pious foundation, generally depended upon a specific grant from him. Buildings, however, also had to bear witness to the glory of God and the beneficence of the Sultan. Other Muslim cultures have had their court architects, but in none was the office more essential than in the Ottoman empire: the evolution of this office, of which Sinan was its most famous holder, is an important theme of this short study.

Sinan was, of course, a Muslim building for Muslim patrons, and the Ottomans were the greatest Muslim empire of their age. How illuminating is it therefore to describe his architecture as Islamic? Certainly it is in the sense that most of his buildings were Muslim religious foundations; but otherwise not much more, it must be said, than describing Sir Christopher Wren's as Christian.

The arts and architecture of Islam are incontestably one of the great adornments of world culture. Yet, to judge from the very little that we know of their practitioners their status was low. Treatises on the arts, in contrast to those of the Roman Vitruvius and his European Renaissance successors, are written by amateurs for amateurs, not for craftsmen, though, unlike the latter, which regard architecture as a superior form of achievement, they do not argue for hierarchies of the arts, or assimilate architecture to music or claim the artist as theoretician or divinely inspired— the sort of thing that, for the writers of the Italian Renaissance, was something to be taken for granted. And in foundation inscriptions that, far more than in European architecture, are a standard feature of Islamic buildings it is generally the founder or his agent who is commemorated. When a craftsman's name appears, moreover, it is often left unclear what he actually did.

To these generalizations Sinan is really no exception. He was a practitioner, not a theoretician, and did not even write a practical treatise. His name appears on none of his many buildings, except in the epitaph on his tomb at Süleymaniye in Istanbul, composed by the poet, Mustafa Sâ'î; and (actually like many architects in other cultures) his responsibilities were so wide that his personal contribution to his many projects is often difficult to assess precisely. Yet even in his lifetime he was famous—the Euclid or the Aristotle of his time, his contemporaries suggested. His fame totally eclipsed his immediate successors, about whom we actually know rather more, and up to the present day his works are regarded in Turkey as the acme of the Ottoman classical style and himself as the paradigm Islamic architect, whose example it would be impious to disregard. The mosques in concrete and corrugated iron erected all over Turkey in the past thirty years or so all pay their debased tribute to him. Not only that: outside Turkey he is the only Islamic architect whose name regularly appears beside the great architects of the European Renaissance and their successors.

That makes Sinan worth a biographical study. Here we come up against a problem. The minimal attention he receives from later sixteenth-century Ottoman historians is exacerbated by the low priority given in Muslim cultures to memoirs and autobiography. In later Ottoman Turkey this was less true, but in Sinan's case the surviving memoirs of his works give little or no idea of his personality. If this is a biography, therefore, it is perforce one of the Court Architect's office in Ottoman Turkey in the age of Sinan and his immediate successors. It is also intended to show how the great projects they directed illustrate their qualifications and training, the functions they fulfilled and their status at the Ottoman Court—higher, probably, than in any other Islamic culture before them and even in contemporary India and Iran.

It might be thought unwise in a study of Ottoman metropolitan architecture of the classical period, in which Justinian's great church of Hagia Sophia, with its rich accumulation of myth, ritual, and symbolism, inevitably plays a major role, to disregard the possibility of symbolism in Sinan's buildings. The problem is that there is nothing *inherently* symbolic in an architect's use of space, and it is very difficult, even when we may know why a building was erected, to decide whether its symbolism is general or specific. In the Ottoman case, we have virtually no direct evidence for the theoretical grounds for the choice of a particular plan, constitution, site, elevation, or decorative scheme—and there may indeed have been none. Nor do we have much evidence for intelligent intervention by patrons at any stage in planning or construction, even though it quite probably did occur at one time or another. Despite some recent claims to the contrary, Sinan, unlike Alberti and Palladio, was not a learned architect; his clients, unlike theirs, were not learned; and his buildings do not therefore reflect a theoretical dialogue. The current vogue for attributing symbolic meaning to Sinan's buildings is, therefore, in my view an anachronism.

This is not, of course, to claim that the grandeur, beauty, or impressiveness of Sinan's works are somehow accidental. The creation of spaces as well as fabrics must always have been at the forefront of his preoccupations, and the viewer was meant to perceive this both from inside and outside, all round if possible or, when buildings were necessarily encapsulated in their surroundings, to come upon the inside as a sudden surprise. Orientation to Makka gives his buildings a directional character, of course, but the central importance of the dome diminishes the importance of axial planning, and where buildings were intended to dominate the horizon the point from which they are viewed may well be immaterial. His greatest buildings may fairly be described as striking the visitor all of a heap, witness the fact that the interiors of Süleymaniye and of Selimiye at Edirne are so resistant to capture by the modern camera lens.

It would be ridiculous, admittedly, to maintain that all the elements of Sinan's buildings—for example, the müezzins' rostrum inside Selimiye at Edirne, which has an ornamental pool underneath it—are perspicuous and self-explanatory. We may never know why that was so curiously situated. But, unsatisfactory as our modern understanding may be, it is not really advanced by concocting a symbolic explanation for its presence there.

Though some of the conclusions suggested here are new and will, I hope, be of interest to historians of Ottoman Turkey and its architecture and architectural decoration this essay is intended for the non-professional. The inevitable residue of abstruse terminology is explained in the Glossary. My debt to earlier scholars is vast. The appearance of their works in the Bibliography is an acknowledgement of what I have learned from them. The most accessible of these are listed in the Further Reading section.

I am grateful to the Research Fund of the School of Oriental and African Studies of the University of London and the British Academy (Humanities Research Board, now Arts and Humanities Research Board) for grants enabling me to work in the Turkish archives, and to the Turkish authorities for permission to do so. The first draft of my text was largely written during a term's Visiting Fellowship at New College, Oxford: I am extremely grateful to the Warden and Fellows for their hospitality.

This study is affectionately dedicated to Christian Hesketh, whose generous hospitality and achievements in the course of a very busy life are an inspiration to all her many friends.

J. M. Rogers

ACKNOWLEDGEMENTS

For permission to reproduce items in their collections, my thanks to: The Trustees of the British Museum, London; The Trustees of the Chester Beatty Library, Dublin; the Director of the Türk Tarih Kurumu, Ankara; the Director of the Topkapı Saray Museum, Istanbul; the Director of the Museum of Turkish and Islamic Art, Istanbul. The line drawings are after originals by the late architect, Ali Saim Ülgen, and I am grateful to the Director of the Türk Tarih Kurumu in Ankara for his permission to use them. And, for their kindness in furnishing photocopies of scarce publications, my thanks to: Dr Ian Jenkins, The British Museum, and Mr Kaveh Bakhtiyar.

Transliteration and place names

I have kept the established English spellings of Turkish or Arabic terms like Pasha, vizier, etc. Where Arabic was unavoidable I have omitted the conventional diacriticals. Where Turkish (see *Glossary*) retains the Arabic *'ayn* I have indicated it with an apostrophe. The inflection marking the construct form (*izafet*) has usually been ignored—Topkapı Saray, not Sarayı; Beglerbeg (modern Beylerbey), not Beglerbegi. Ottoman Turkish is given in its modernized (simplified) Turkish form where the only diacritical used is the circumflex accent for long vowels. Modern Turkish is a more or less phonetic rendering of the language in Romanized script, with additional vowels (ı, ö and ü) and consonants (c [j], ç [ch], ğ [gh], j [zh], and ş [sh]). These characters appear in Turkish dictionaries as distinct entries: however, in the Index here, Ç appears under C, etc. The dotted i in upper case (İ) has been ignored throughout.

For Islamic calendar dates in the Ottoman sources I have, where appropriate, also given their Western equivalents. Byzantine and Ottoman place names very often differ not only from one another but from modern toponymy, both in the former provinces of the Ottoman empire and in Turkish Anatolia. As a general rule, the current forms are given, but with the older form in brackets where this is also in common use. Some inconsistency is regrettable but inevitable, for example, Hagia Sophia for Justinian's great church but Ayasofya for the district of Istanbul that it dominates.

Note on sources

Although Sinan, to his contemporaries no less than his successors, was the superlative genius among Ottoman architects, the literary and archival sources for his life and works are poor. He is rarely mentioned by contemporary historians and is totally ignored by the European travellers of his time, though they sometimes depict his major buildings in Istanbul. On the other hand, the later seventeenth-century traveller Evliyâ Çelebi's account of his works is notoriously uncritical. Contemporary documents in the Turkish National Archives in Istanbul (the Başbakanlık Arşivi, BBA) in which he and his staff occasionally appear include registers of maintenance and repairs to the Imperial monuments in Istanbul (mostly in the Maliyeden Müdevver series, MM/MAD); registers of honoraria and gratuities to Court officials (*in'âmât* or *mevâcib* defters); and summaries of Imperial orders, the so-called registers of important matters (Mühimme defters, MD). Unfortunately, these series contain many gaps and it is never possible to follow the progress of the works Sinan supervised from planning to realization. Most of what we can say about Sinan as a practising architect, therefore, has to be deduced from his buildings.

Additional sources, however, which give considerable information on works by, associated with, or attributed to Sinan, are three lists of his buildings compiled towards the end of his life, or just after his death. These are the *Tezkiretü'l-Bünyân* (dedicated to Siyavuş Pasha, Grand Vizier 1582–4) and the *Tezkiretü'l-Ebniye*, both by Mustafa Sâ'î Çelebi (d. 1004/1595–6) and the latter dictated to him, he says, by Sinan; and the anonymous *Tuhfetü'l-Mi'mârîn* (probably datable to the 1590s). The autograph of the first, in the library of Süleymaniye in Istanbul, Hacı Mahmud Efendi 4911, bears some notes not in Sâ'î's hand, mostly relating to expenditure. They may or not be in Sinan's own hand, but later copyists evidently thought they were, for they incorporated them into the text. These three lists, however, give very different estimates of their numbers: taken together they amount to 477 projects, 314 in all three accounts; 40 in two of them; and 123 in only one. Deciding which estimate to accept is thus sometimes a difficult matter.

Ottoman Turkey in the age of Sinan
The political and military background

On 29 May 1453 the Ottoman Sultan Mehmed II captured Constantinople and with the capture in 1461 of Trebizond, the last refuge of the Comnene emperors, put an end to more than a thousand years of Byzantine rule. The already powerful Ottoman state became an empire, or rather, as Mehmed II himself thought, two empires: the bastion of Islam against Europe and the East; and the heir of Byzantium. The palaces he built, his repopulation of the city with the inhabitants of many cities in the Ottoman provinces, and the building of a great complex, Fâtih, with his mosque at its centre began the transformation of the Byzantine capital into an imperial Muslim city (henceforth it was more usually known as Istanbul). But his patronage of artists and writers, Persian, Turkish, Greek, and even Italian, deservedly merits comparison with European Renaissance contemporaries. With the further capture of Caffa in the Crimea (1475) he ousted the Genoese from their hitherto unchallenged maritime supremacy in the Black Sea, and his attacks on the Eastern Mediterranean Venetian colonies were to lead in the sixteenth century to Ottoman maritime domination there too.

The city that Mehmed captured had in the last centuries of Byzantium undergone such decline that it barely merited the name of capital. His first decision was to transform the church of Hagia Sophia into his Great Mosque by having evening prayers said there on the day of its capture. To it in 861/1457 all the standing Byzantine churches of the city were made *vakf*, together with baths, shops, the principal covered market (the Bedesten), and the great wholesale warehouses in the harbour areas on the Golden Horn. His complex, Fâtih, completed early in 1471 on the site of the ruined Byzantine Patriarchate, with eight large *medreses* and other appurtenances, was not only to become the centre where the judges and administrators of the Ottoman state were trained but set the example to his viziers and other officials, to whom grants of the various quarters of the Byzantine city had been made, to transform them into Muslim areas with mosques and their dependencies at their centre. Coherence was maintained through their links with the main thoroughfare, the Divan Yolu, and the harbour areas on the Golden Horn; significantly, the old alignments were preserved as far as possible by Court Architects even when rebuilding after serious fires.

Mehmed II died in 1481. His successor, Bayazid II, who is praised by the historians above all for his piety, was something of a consolidator. During his reign political and administrative centralization increased, and both the army and the navy were reformed. The artillery was built up and the army was equipped with muskets, which ensured the Ottoman victories of the early sixteenth century over the Persians and then over the Mamluks in Egypt and Syria. Between 1499 and 1502 the navy was even to challenge the Venetian fleet on the open seas. Stability favoured economic development and Bayazid's foundations in Istanbul and at Edirne, which proclaimed its status as the second city of the Ottoman empire, were the most splendid of their time.

On the Eastern front in the very early sixteenth century the rise to power of the Safavids in Iran, a Turkish-speaking dynasty but with fiercely nationalistic Shi'i ambitions, polarized the conflict between Sunnis and the Shi'a. Their defeat at the hands of Bayazid's successor, Selim I (1512–20), at Çaldıran in late summer of 1514 brought Eastern Anatolia under Ottoman rule, though hostilities were to continue well into the seventeenth century. Selim's conquest of Syria in 1516 and then of Egypt and the Hijaz in 1517 gave the Ottomans primacy in Sunni Islam. Control over the richest centres of the transit trade created the prosperity that set Süleyman the Magnificent (1520–66) and his successors Selim II (1566–74) and Murad III (1574–95) in their dominant position in European, even world, politics. Up to 1596, the distinguished historian of Ottoman Turkey Halil Inalcık has concluded, there was no international question in Europe that, at least indirectly, did not involve the Ottomans.

Süleyman the Magnificent's role as a European statesman was facilitated by the persistent rivalry between the French and the Habsburg emperor Charles V and his successors. He mostly favoured the French, while the Protestant princes of Germany were a useful counterweight to the Holy Roman Empire. This enabled him to juggle his alliances so that he did not have to fight simultaneously on the European and the Safavid fronts. European divisions, moreover, effectively frustrated the crusades preached by successive Popes. The one occasion on which an alliance of European powers inflicted a major defeat on the Ottomans was the battle of Lepanto (1571) in which the Ottoman fleet was destroyed, but despite that serious reverse the Ottoman fleet was rebuilt in a year and Cyprus captured by Selim II in 1572. It is fortunate, as Aptullah Kuran says, that Sinan's development coincided with the great expansion of the Ottoman empire and a multitude of high-placed patrons that gave him ample budgets and made rapid execution, even for the greatest buildings, a reality.

On one front the Ottomans and the European powers were united: fear of Portuguese expansion in the Indian Ocean, which threatened an Eastern empire based upon a monopoly of the spice trade via the Cape of Good Hope. But although the Ottoman navy was overstretched the monopoly never materialized. North of the Danube and on the Black Sea the Ottomans were less successful in preventing the expansion of Muscovy. By the time Murad III came to the throne, moreover, the increasing cost of men, munitions, and supplies in more or less continuous campaigns against the Safavids was beginning to tell. This led contemporaries to the belief that the dynasty was in decline and to see nostalgically the reign of Süleyman the Magnificent as a classical age. The supposed decline was, however, an anticipation of what occurred much later, and the Ottoman achievement in the age of Sinan is by any criteria impressive.

THE JANISSARIES AND THE PALACE SCHOOL

From its origins the Ottoman state had been a military institution, with a fundamental distinction between those who paid tax, merchants, peasants, and craftsmen (re'âyâ), and those in the service of the state (askerî), who did not. The military were charged with maintaining order in the villages, fortresses, and towns of the fiefs (timars) they had been assigned, and the tax revenues from them were their pay. In return, they were subject to campaign service. Though a provincial hereditary nobility never really came into being, the system may be described, not too misleadingly, as 'feudal'.

The military administration of provincial commanders and the religious administration of judges headed by two Military Judges (Kazasker, Kadıasker), of Turkey in Europe (Rumeli) and Anatolia, developed in parallel, though by 1500 the Grand Vizier was practically always chosen from the military, and the other viziers too. The Sultan's council (Dîvân-ı Hümâyûn), which advised him, represented him during his absence on campaign, and served as a court of appeal, included the viziers, the two Kadıaskers, the head of the Treasury (Defterdâr), and the head of the Chancery (Nişâncı).

The provincial landholders (the Sipahis) were mostly cavalry. The Sultans' household troops (Kapıkulları) comprised infantry, the Janissaries, and a household cavalry, to which in the later fifteenth century were added regiments of armourers and heavy artillery. The Janissaries, who were armed with muskets, had by Mehmed II's accession gained a formidable reputation in the Balkans and in Eastern Anatolia.

The Ottomans were one of several Turkish dynasties that had slave armies, but they certainly carried the principle further in making slave (*kul*) status a major requirement for the highest office. This term was sometimes also used for anyone apart from the royal family who belonged to the ruling institution, in any capacity from gardener to grand vizier, and even for the feudal Sipahis, who did not receive pay from the Sultan; here 'servants' might be a better translation. But the highest military–administrative officials had all originated as slaves, and along the line of their promotion never seem to have undergone any formal manumission.

The most famous of the Ottoman slave corps were the Janissaries, an infantry who, from the names of their regiments, very probably derived from huntsmen attached to the Sultan. They were originally formed of the statutory one-fifth of prisoners that fell to the Sultan's lot as slaves, supplemented by purchases in the markets and by gifts from petitioners to the Sultan. The notorious recruiting practice through periodic levies of Christian boys (the *devşirme*) seems to have been adopted during the reign of Murad II (d. 1451) during a lull in the flow of prisoners of war. These levies were subject to numerous exemptions; there are some exceptions to practically every generalization, and the system was in constant evolution: it is dangerous, therefore, to read back practice in the seventeenth or the later sixteenth centuries, which is generally better documented, into the reigns of Bayazid II and Selim I. Since the losses by war were sometimes considerable the average annual renewal may have been as much as a tenth of the total slave army, which has been estimated at eighty thousand. On the other hand, in more settled times the levy may have occurred only once every few years.

The levies were preponderantly from the European provinces of Turkey—Bulgaria, Greece, Serbia, Macedonia, Bosnia-Herzegovina, and Albania (and Hungary as well after it fell into Turkish hands in the reign of Süleyman the Magnificent)—and hence were mostly of Orthodox Christians, in spite of the fact that Islam prohibits the forced conversion of protected minorities. The boys were almost exclusively from rural populations, and since the levies often deprived them of the best of their able-bodied peasants they were often unpopular with the Turkish feudal landholders. In Anatolia they were restricted to the provinces of Trebizond (Trabzon), Karaman, Erzurum, and Kayseri. The writer Koçi Beg allows that Armenians qualified for the devşirme, but Georgians, it seems, did not, though many of these were purchased in the slave markets of Istanbul to swell the numbers of the Janissary privates (Acemioğlans).

The boys, whose ages ranged from 10 to 20 (perhaps with a bias towards those who were older, with a view to standardizing the training they received), were selected from the baptismal registers, carefully inspected by experienced officials for any defects, and taken to Istanbul where they underwent formal conversion to Islam. Yet another inspection took place, and those who were most presentable, physically and intellectually, were selected as pages (İçoğlans) for training in special colleges like the Galata Saray (founded under Bayazid II). The remainder were assigned to households of feudal Sipahi landholders, to learn Turkish and work on the land, and on completing their training were drafted as private soldiers into the Janissaries or the Bostancıs (initially, the corps of gardeners). Most of the latter then learned military trades (armourers, saddlers, washermen, or surgeons) and became responsible for the administration of the transport, commissariat, and artillery corps, or the Imperial stables. Yet others were drafted to work in naval dockyards, particularly at Gallipoli on the Dardanelles. Indeed, the Acemioğlans when not on campaign functioned as a reservoir of unskilled labour for State works, as at Süleymaniye where the transport of the building materials, often from far distant parts, was largely in their hands. Failure to be selected for the higher schools was not necessarily a permanent disqualification. Distinguished service in the Janissaries could also be rewarded by promotion into the regular cavalry (the Sipahis) with the accompanying grant of a timar.

Prior to the reign of Murad II there is no evidence that the Palace pages (İçoğlans) received more than a military training. With the expansion of the Ottoman empire, however, and the need not merely for soldiers but for administrators, the curriculum for these recruits expanded, probably modelled on the training given the Princes or Şehzades who were posted with their tutors to provincial capitals to prepare them to rule—should they be fortunate enough to reach the throne. Under Mehmed II there may have been as many as 400 pages inside the Palace (*Enderûn*). In the palace at Edirne and the Galata Saray in Istanbul (*Bîrûn*), which were rather less prestigious, there were 300 each.

In addition to sports, archery, fencing, and horsemanship, the pages were taught a modicum of theology, religious and administrative law, and often mastered Arabic and Persian, as well as Ottoman Turkish. Some, like the Albanian Taşlıcalı Yahya, were poets and some practised calligraphy, though evidently as a diversion: they were too valuable to disappear into the Ottoman Civil Service. Some with an aptitude for finance or the secretariat were ultimately appointed to the Chancery, while Bayazid II is known to have encouraged those with a talent for the religious sciences (Arabic *'ilm*) to join the clerisy (*ilmiyye*). The palace pages were divided for administrative purposes into two groups, the Greater and the Lesser Chambers (*Büyük Oda, Küçük Oda*). On passing out, at an average age of 25, and after yet another review (it would not be anachronistic to describe their education as 'continuous assessment'), the top forty were assigned to attendance upon the Sultan in the Privy Chamber (*Hasoda*) for a further four years.

The *Bîrûn* was very largely staffed by graduates from the *Enderûn*, just as the provincial administration of France under De Gaulle and Pompidou was largely in the hands of the 'Énarques', graduates of the École Nationale d'Administration. In the provinces, however, their colleagues also included the freeborn sons of Ottoman officials, men who may have served in other households, or even freeborn peasants (*re'âyâ*) who had served with distinction in the Sultan's campaigns. Nor, in terms of values, level of education, and refinement, was there a profound distinction between those trained in the Palace or those in private households. However, although men of varied origins served in most ranks of the military–administrative system the highest office, that of Grand Vizier, seems to have been exclusively a slave appointment.

Janissary pay registers show, in fact, that rather more Ottoman officials were sons of Muslim fathers, hence freeborn, than this picture might suggest. It was an accepted principle that sons of Ottoman officers qualified for posts in the administration after their father's death or retirement, though generally at a much lower level, receiving a fief of only 5–10 per cent of their father's. A few sons of Ottoman officials also entered the Palace service, in the Bîrûn, as *Müteferrika*, the Sultan's 'noble guard' which also included princely tributaries, their salaries being paid directly by the Treasury, some by larger fiefs (*ze'âmet*), and some by annual stipends. Though with time their numbers increased they were never so numerous as to compete with the graduates of the Palace schools, nor does the Court Architect ever appear to have been among them.

2

Sinan

The great sixteenth century Ottoman Court Architect, whose Muslim name may have been Yûsuf, is generally known as Sinan, probably a contraction of the sobriquet (*lakab*) Sinânuddîn ('Steel spearhead of the Faith'). 'Sinan' is a common name in Janissary registers in sixteenth-century Turkey. Not only was the Court Architect of Mehmed the Conqueror a Sinan—Âzâdlı Sinan (the Freedman) or Sinan-ı Atîk (the Elder)—in an account book for repairs to the palace at Edirne dated 1556-7, for example, in which Sinan himself was certainly involved, there was a Sinan who was Ağa of the Palace (Comptroller of the Royal Household), a Sinan who was head of the Imperial masons, and a Sinan who was head of the Bostancıs, the Janissary troops responsible for the maintenance of the palace grounds. Even more confusingly, at the time the architect Sinan was involved with the construction of Süleymaniye (inaugurated 1557) his Clerk of the Works (*binâ emîni*) was a Sinan Beg. In virtue of his architectural appointment he is generally referred to in contemporary documents as Sinan Ağa, rather than Sinan Beg, a title of major fief-holders and military governors; but these titles are somewhat inconsistently applied.

The sources for Sinan's life and career are few, and almost entirely on the Ottoman side. Though sixteenth century illustrations of Istanbul by foreign travellers show some of his buildings, notably Süleymaniye in Melchior Lorichs's panorama of 1557 [Fig. 1],

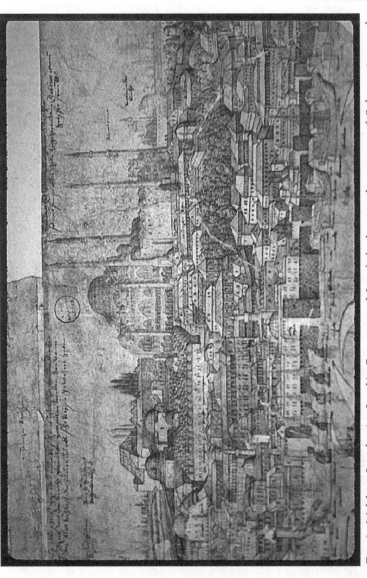

Fig. 1. Melchior Lorichs (or Lorck), Panorama of Istanbul, showing the mosque of Süleymaniye on the skyline. Leiden, University Library. After E. Oberhummer, Constantinopel unter Sultan Suleiman dem Grossen (Munich, 1902).

no traveller's account mentions him or describes them. His status in the later decades of his life as the preeminent architect of his time was unchallenged, but he established no dynasty: indeed, although the text of his endowment deed (*vakfiye*) names his wife, a son (deceased), two daughters and a grandson, and a nephew and two great-nieces among the beneficiaries (these last three indicating that his brother also was a convert to Islam), his brother's career and their fate remain obscure. Nor is Sinan often mentioned in contemporary historical chronicles.

Although the Ottoman archives may still have details to contribute, the few facts relating to his life and career can be compressed into little more than a page. Born c.1490 of a Turkish-speaking Christian family from Ağırnas in the province of Kayseri in Cappadocia, he was conscripted into the Janissaries, probably in his late teens, with the name of Sinan b. Abdülmennan (like Abdullah, a common patronymic in Ottoman Turkey for Christian converts to Islam). Like quite a lot of *devşirme* boys he did not lose contact with his family. He endowed a fountain (*çeşme*) at Ağırnas, and in 1573 his petition to the Sublime Porte that his family should not be deported with the rest of the town to repopulate the island of Cyprus—which had been conquered by Selim II the previous year—was granted, on the grounds that he himself was an inhabitant of Ağırnas.[1]

Sinan partly owed his accelerated promotion to the heavy mortality of the period 1512–20, on Selim I's Çaldıran campaign of 1514 and his conquest of Syria and Egypt in 1516–17, on which he may or may not have served. Subsequently, in the words of Mustafa Sâ'î's *Tezkiretü'l-Bünyân*, he took part in Süleyman the Magnificent's attacks on Rhodes and Belgrade (1521), and then in the Mohács (1526), Vienna (1529), Iraq (1534–35), Corfu (1537), Apulia and Moldavia (1538) campaigns. The inclusion of Corfu and Apulia suggests that he was part of the amphibious forces. From 1523–6 he was an Atlı Sekban (a mounted Janissary officer); after Mohács he was promoted to Yayabaşı (an Infantry captain)

[1]Dated 7 Ramazan 981/31 Jan. 1574 [Refik 1977, no. 23].

and then to Zemberekçibaşı (Commander of the Crossbowmen, though by this time the Janissaries were armed with muskets), commanding the 82nd Janissary unit (*ocak*); on the return from Iraq in 1535 he was made Haseki (roughly, a Sergeant at Arms of the Imperial guard). Shortly after his appointment as Court Architect in 1537, following the death of Acem Ali, he joined the Moldavian campaign of 1538. This was at the recommendation of Lutfi Pasha, later Second Vizier, who—possibly on account of a bath he built for him in the district of Yenibağçe in Istanbul in 1536—described him as a highly experienced architect (*mi'mâr-i kârdân*). He was also granted Acem Ali's fief (*arpalık*) of Torilye and its surrounding villages from the Sultan's own estates in the sancak of Vize in Turkish Thrace. This *arpalık* was in 1216/1802 still the prerogative of the Court Architect, producing, however, the comparatively minor sum of 8883 akçe per annum.

Sinan's distinguished military career suggests that he had attended one of the schools for pages, where his technical training was in carpentry (which evidently implied construction rather than joinery), from which he would have graduated to the maintenance and repair of military installations. He may or may not have built a wooden bridge for Lutfi Pasha over the River Pruth in 13 days on the Moldavian campaign—more of an achievement than it sounds since it had to bear heavy artillery, as well as all the loaded wagons of equipment and supplies—but he had almost certainly supervised the great stone bridge at Uzunköprü (Svilengrad in Bulgaria) built in 935/1528–9 for Çoban Mustafa Pasha, as part of the preparations for Süleyman the Magnificent's advance on Vienna in 1529. The repairs associated with Süleyman the Magnificent's campaigns became steadily more substantial, culminating in the restoration of the shrines of Abu Hanifa and 'Abd al-Qadir al-Gilani at Baghdad in the wake of his campaign against the Safavids of 1534–5, though they were subsequently rebuilt in Persian Safavid style and no traces remain of Süleyman's restoration. These were built of brick, but only such works are consonant with the scale of Sinan's Istanbul debut, the complex of Süleyman the Magnificent's wife, Haseki Hürrem Sultan (946/

1539–40). Even so, he does not appear to have spent any time working in the Court Architect's office before his appointment, which he probably owed to the intervention of Lutfî Pasha. For he is conspicuously absent from a list of Court Architects (dated Rebi'ülevvel 943/September–October 1536)[2], with Alauddin Ali (Acem Ali) still at their head, which included an Italian, Françesko Kapudan, whose distinction is indicated by the wish, *Nuvvira bakâ'uhu!* (roughly, May his career be brilliant!) and whom Sinan evidently displaced.

It would be unreasonable to expect any great originality from the mosque of Haseki Hürrem Sultan, which follows that of Çoban Mustafa Pasha at Gebze (930/1522–3)—not one of Sinan's buildings. The rest of her complex developed more slowly: the plan of its *medrese* (946/1539–40) is modelled on the medical school of Bayazid II at Edirne. Its *imaret* (Rebî'ülâhır 957/April–May 1550), ordered by Süleyman the Magnificent, is not attributed to Sinan in any of the sources, though he may have been responsible for the hospital added in *c*.1550–8.

WATERWORKS AND THE INSPECTORATE OF WATERWORKS (SUYOLU NÂZIRLIĞI)

An essential preliminary to any imperial Ottoman building project was the installation of a piped water supply. At the outset of Sinan's career as Court Architect the Inspectorate of Waterworks had not yet become a separate post. He was thus responsible for repairs and maintenance of the major elements, dams, cisterns, and aqueducts, of the water supplies he planned for his foundations. But, in Istanbul at least, they would have been of little use without a master plan for the distribution of the water inside the city, with mains distribution points (*taksim/maksem*), and hydraulic balances (*su teraziyeleri*) or inverted syphons, as at the Aqueduct of Valens, to cope with the unpredictable side effects of increased demand. These matters involved complex calculations, as well as estimates

[2]BBA MM/MAD 559, Ramazan 942–Zilhicce 943/late Feb. 1536–Jun. 1537.

of future consumption, and certainly took as much of Sinan's time as his architectural projects. This master plan must have been no less essential when the post of Inspector of Waterworks was created in 1566, though under Sinan's successors adaptations or improvements were certainly made. Contemporary plans of Ottoman watercourses were made to facilitate repairs and maintenance, showing collection points, dams, aqueducts, tunnels, mains distribution points, and syphons, and these include a sketch map of one of Süleyman's waterworks, the Kâğıthane system on the outskirts of Istanbul in the *Süleymânnâme* in the Chester Beatty Library in Dublin, a panegyric history ordered by Murad III in the 1580s [Fig. 2].

Though the post of Inspector of Waterworks was established only in 1566 when Hasan Ağa, a pupil of Sinan's, was appointed, at least two years previously members of the Court Architect's office were evidently specializing in this branch of works. Late in 1564 a Greek engineer, Kosta, responsible for the water supply to the fortress of Aya Mavra, on the island of Levkas in the Ionian Islands, was rebuked by the central authorities for exceeding his instructions: the water was piped underground from a spring on Levkas and then carried across the lagoon to the fortress by an aqueduct of 366 arches, a distance of three kilometres in all and a major feat of engineering. Instead, however, of taking the water inside the fortress and providing for the Sipahi garrison he stopped it at the houses outside it, on the grounds that the provision for fountains was grossly inadequate and that in fact they required the greater part of the flow.[3] Kosta evidently argued his case convincingly, for later his daily stipend was increased.

The Inspectorate of Waterworks evidently came to be seen as a stepping stone to higher office: Sinan's immediate successors, Davud Ağa, Dalgıç Ahmed Pasha, and Mehmed Ağa all held the post before being appointed Court Architect. Like the position of Court Architect the post entitled the holder to a military fief: Hasan Ağa was granted the *arpalık* of several villages in Thrace,

[3]BBA *MD* 6, p.129 no.273, 17 Rabî'ülevvel 972/24 Oct. 1564.

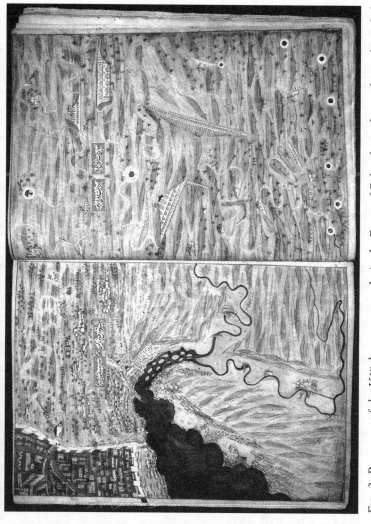

FIG. 2. *Panorama of the Kâğıthane waterworks in the Forest of Belgrade on the outskirts of Istanbul. From the Süleymanname of Seyyid Lokman (987/1579). Dublin, Chester Beatty Library MS 413, folios 22ᵇ–23ᵃ.*

while Davud Ağa was the holder of a *ze'âmet*. Vital as Sinan's expertise in waterworks had been, however, his responsibilities in this sphere may have been largely confined to Istanbul. For the feasibility study for a canal from the Mediterranean to the Red Sea, planned by Sokollu Mehmed Pasha in 1568 but later abandoned, was entrusted to the Commander-in-Chief (*Beglerbeg*) of Egypt. And if Sinan was consulted over Selim II's most grandiose project, the building of a canal from the Don to the Volga in 1569 to enable an attack on Astrakhan, his advice was not followed, for it was a total fiasco.

Sinan does appear to have been consulted on another such project, for a canal to join the River Sakarya to Lake Sapanca and thence to the Gulf of Izmid at the eastern end of the Sea of Marmara, with a view to building a naval dockyard (*tersane*) on the lake, providing water for Izmid and its surroundings, creating new pastures by drainage and controlling flooding in the Sakarya plain, and easing supplies of grain, firewood, timber, and marble from north-west Anatolia to Istanbul. According to the historian Selânikî Mustafa his first attempt, in association with a 'well known' Christian, Nikola Kerez, who had probably worked with him on the Kırkçeşme waterworks (*c.*1554–64) came to nothing. In 990/1582 he was appointed, together with an astrologer and two experts in waterworks, to conduct a feasibility study and mobilize labour, but evidently his report was discouraging, for, when the project was taken up again in 1591 after his death, after three months of works it was suddenly abandoned.

Sinan's Imperial waterworks fall into three groups: (i) the Taşlımüsellim system at Edirne; (ii) the Süleymaniye system, the Halkalı Suyu (known later as the Mîrî or Beylik Suyu), completed, probably, by 1557; and (iii) the Kırkçeşme system, completed perhaps by 1564. The first of these, according to Peçevî, was completed in 936/1529–30 in connection with a mosque founded by Süleyman the Magnificent's wife, Haseki Hürrem at the bridge built over the River Meriç (Maritsa) in Thrace (Uzunköprü, now Svilengrad in Bulgaria) by the vizier Çoban Mustafa Pasha. This was extended in 961/1554 to cope with new palace buildings at Edirne and provide for the irrigation of the palace gardens across the River Tunca. Whether this aqueduct would have reached the courtyard fountain of Selimiye at the time works began on the site is, however, uncertain: if it did not predate them its further extension must have involved considerable modifications in the course of the works.

Despite remains, partly still in working order, of both Roman and Byzantine waterworks in the environs of Edirne and Istanbul, the vast increase in water consumption by the Imperial foundations for which Sinan was responsible entailed radical modifications. Inside Istanbul this presented particular difficulty, for the ground water was mostly brackish and already far from sufficient for public needs, so that the additional strain created by the new Imperial foundations could well have caused public unrest. He set to work on the Halkalı system, which was originally Hadrianic (117–38 AD), with additions by Valens (364–78 AD), whose aqueduct *intra muros* is dated 368 AD, and later by Justinian. In the Middle and Late Byzantine periods, doubtless with the secular decrease in population, there had been a move from aqueducts to open or covered cisterns inside the walls. These still remained in use. The Ottomans as Hanafi Muslims, however, were obliged to make their ablutions in running water: hence the complex system of aqueducts and tunnels, which Mehmed II adopted among his measures to repopulate the city after the conquest of 1453. Sinan's extension of the system, which channelled two of the upper branches of the Sweet Waters of Europe (Kâğıthane Suyu), in the Forest of Belgrade to the north of Istanbul involved major construction, and four aqueducts are attributed to him in the *Tezkiretü'l-Ebniye*: the Uzun/Petnahor, the Eğri/Kovuk, the Mağlova/ Muğlava (possibly the most impressive) and the Güzelce/Gözlüce aqueducts [Fig. 3].[4] A late sixteenth century plan of the Halkalı

---

[4]In a contemporary panegyric account of Süleyman the Magnificent's reign, the *Menâkıb-ı Sultân Süleymân* by the poet Eyyûbî (cf. Akkuş, 1991, 191–2), the officials credited with the work are, first, the Ağa or Commander of the Janissaries and, secondly, the Admiral of the Fleet, the Kapudan Paşa, who together evidently commanded the labour force. Eyyûbî praises the architect

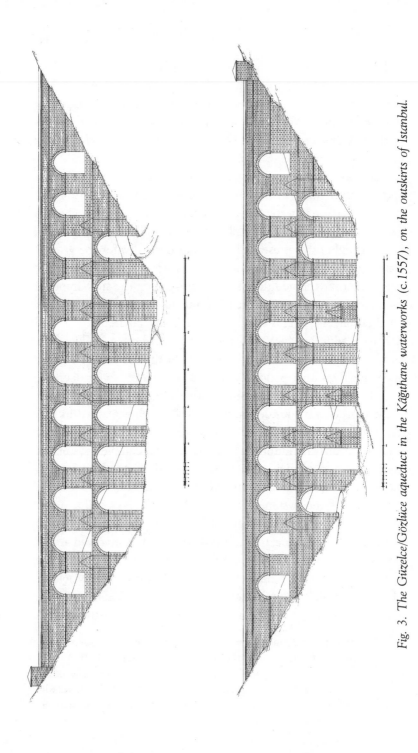

Fig. 3. The Güzelce/Gözlüce aqueduct in the Kâğıthane waterworks (c.1557), on the outskirts of Istanbul.

system in the Topkapı Saray archives drawn up by Davud Ağa indicates precisely the amount of water to be drawn by pious foundations inside the walls of Istanbul, and the Old and the New Palaces as well.

The Kırkçeşme system, which was more closely linked with Süleymaniye, may also have been reconstructed as early as Mehmed II's reign, but was largely rebuilt between 1554 and 1563, following serious flood damage. According to Sâ'î, it was restored and enlarged the following year, providing more than 300 fountains inside Istanbul (*yapıldı çeşme üçyüzden ziyade*) at a cost of 40 million akçe, repairs and maintenance costing an extra 9 million. Compared with the *total* building costs of Süleymaniye, about 55 million akçe, the fountains could hardly be said to have come cheap.[5] The expenditure was, however, almost certainly deliberate, to forestall public unrest, for the waterworks for the Sultans' own foundations were, in their view private works and the public had no access to them.

The volume of the original water supply of Süleymaniye at its inauguration is unknown, but with additions of the 1560s could have been as much as two and a half gallons a second. Given the proximity of Süleymaniye to Şehzade, the authorities may initially have thought that its water supply would suffice for both. Sinan must have had to make the crucial decision to demand another system right at the outset of works. A recent survey[6] of the water distribution inside the complex of Süleymaniye by Ali Saim Ülgen, based partly on sixteenth-/eighteenth-century charts [Fig. 4], illustrates his methods. The water supply entered the walled garden of the mosque from the main distribution point (*taksim*) near its south corner. Pipes led straight to the *şadırvan* at the centre of the courtyard, which, we learn from

---

in extravagant terms; but not by name and only in third place. He must have been writing, however, with patronage in view and Admirals and Commanders-in-Chief were a much better prospect for a poet than the Court Architect.

[5]However, the reconstruction of the Mağlova aqueduct in 1563 was even more expensive, over 50 million akçe (Saatçı 1991).

[6]Çeçen 1986.

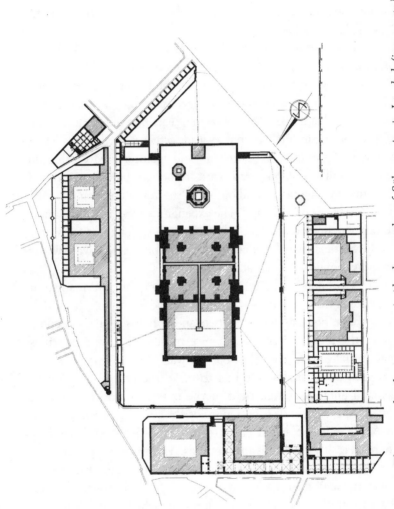

Fig. 4. The water distribution system inside the complex of Süleymaniye in Istanbul (inaugurated in 1557).

the *Tuhfetü'l-Mi'mârîn*, was filled from the roof and which served as a reservoir from which other pipes conveyed water to the peripheral blocks of the complex. These are all rather shallow and could easily have been laid once the buildings of the complex were substantially complete. With the exception of the Third and Fourth *medreses* they do not seem to have been taken inside them, however.

The location of the central internal distribution point at the *şadırvan* in the centre of the mosque courtyard and the siting of the ablutions at the base of the side walls outside must have been Sinan's first decisions in the Süleymaniye project. The *şadırvan* was placed at the crossing of deep tunnels dug on the axes of the courtyard. That on the main axis went from the principal gateway into the walled garden across the courtyard and as far as the centre of the mosque where it forked at right angles to supply the taps for the ablutions built into the outer side walls. In addition short branches also at right angles led to two of the great piers of the mosque for water to wash the floor. He must also simultaneously have decided on a separate drainage system, which has yet to be investigated. The need to plan from the start also had implications for the elevation of the building: the incorporation of the ablutions of Süleymaniye into the outside walls was a conspicuous novelty in Ottoman mosque design.

Curiously, the Süleymaniye *vakfiye* contained no provision for a public fountain (*sebil* or *çeşme*), which Sinan himself had to petition to add in 1587, the expense being met from the surplus revenue of the endowments. Documents published by Ahmed Refik suggest that planning and construction of the complex system of collection tanks and distribution points took at least a decade and that there was constant improvization. Only two years after the inauguration of Süleymaniye in 1557, for example, there were complaints that the flow was inadequate. Much worse, in 1577 Sinan, though ultimately found not guilty of damaging the foundation, was brought to court for tapping the principal water supply of Süleymaniye[7] for a fountain at the door of his house nearby and for building a bath, a cistern, and a basin inside. Evidently by that stage the water supply was so sparse that even a slight overloading caused an inconvenient shortage.

THE COURT ARCHITECTS (HÂSSA MI'MARLARI) AND THEIR OFFICE

Unlike the Inspectorate of Waterworks, the post of Court Architect had its risks, as its holders knew from the story retold in Nizâmî's *Khamsa* of Simnar, the legendary architect of Nu'man, the Lakhmid ruler of Yemen (d. 418 AD), who built the castle of Khawarnaq for him and whom he put to death for fear that he might later excel it. The penalties for failure or disobedience to the Sultan's command were also horrendous. We may be disinclined to believe Evliyâ Çelebi's assertion that Mehmed II chopped off the hands of his Court Architect, Sinan Yûsuf (Âzâdlı Sinan), on the grounds that he had lopped the columns of the mosque of Fâtih and thus failed to surpass Hagia Sophia in height, but the fact remains that he was held guilty of dereliction sufficient to justify his summary execution in September 1471. His example doubtless encouraged his successors.

A constant feature of the Court Architect's office from the reign of Süleyman the Magnificent onwards was the number of non-Muslims it included. Of the fourteen architects named for the Transcaucasian campaign of 1582[8] nine were non-Muslim; though here the urgency of recruiting them may have led to a relaxation in qualifications, religion was thus not necessarily a bar to service in military corps. Up to the mid-nineteenth century, however, no Court Architects seem to have been non-Muslim, though some non-Muslims were promoted to Deputy Court Architect.

[7]BBA *MD 31*, p. 250 no. 551, 1 Receb 985/14 Sept.1577.
[8]BBA *MD 44*, p.131 no. 244, 25 Zilhicce 990/10 Jan. 1583.

Very little is known, apart from their names, of the Court Architects before Sinan, and very few buildings bear their signatures. If the mosque of Selimiye in Istanbul (probably completed in 929/autumn 1522) was the work of Süleyman's first Court Architect, Ali the Persian (Acem Ali), who may have been brought from Tabriz in the aftermath of the battle of Çaldıran by Selim I in 1514, the other buildings that have been credited to him by one writer or another justify Goodwin's judgement of him as an architectural magpie par excellence—though this versatility in a style and techniques completely alien to a Persian-trained master suggests that he was also a remarkable parrot. The plan of the mosque of Selimiye in Istanbul (completed 1522) is very comparable to that of Bayazid II's mosque at Edirne (1485); but though its dome is as large as that of the Üç Şerefeli mosque at Edirne, it is structurally highly conservative and suggests the exaggerated caution of a military engineer who was a novice at mosque construction. Sinan's buildings of the 1540s graphically show how much progress he had made on Ali's works, but in one respect Ali's choice of site, an artificial platform high above the Golden Horn on one side and the open Byzantine cistern of Aspar on the other, was an inspiration for Sinan's sensitivity to topography.

For further information on the Court Architects' training and responsibilities we must therefore consider the careers of Sinan's immediate successors, despite the danger of anachronism because of changes in the organization of the office and the need to take account of their very different personalities. On the other hand, it is also very likely that the additional qualifications that came to be demanded of Court Architects were the direct result of Sinan's personal experience and were an attempt to make his office more efficient. By the time of his death in 996/1588 such measures may have been urgent; his extreme longevity must have greatly complicated the choice of his successor. It also smacks of gerontocracy: his departure for the Hajj in 1584 might have been a prelude to graceful retirement, but on his return, already well into his nineties, he energetically took up work again, probably completing the Hacı Ivaz mosque and the Molla Çelebi mosque at Fındıklı in the remaining four years of his life.

Sinan was succeeded by Davud Ağa. He first appears in 1575 as Inspector of Waterworks in charge of the Kâğıthane system, but two years later was an architect on Sinan's staff. In 1582 he was a Çavuş (herald, pursuivant, or usher at the Imperial Court, an appointment that had nothing specifically to do with architecture); and in 1584 he was Kaldırımcı Çavuş, in charge of the maintenance of the paved roads of Istanbul. In that year when Mehmed, the architect then in charge of Murad III's mosque at Manisa, was made Sinan's deputy during his absence on the Pilgrimage, Davud Ağa was working on the mosque of the head of the Black Eunuchs (Kızlarağası), Mehmed Ağa (completed 993/1585) at Kocamustafapaşa in Istanbul.

As in all Court appointments the succession may not have been entirely a matter of talent, though Davud Ağa's qualifications were not necessarily inferior to Sinan's at the time *he* was appointed Court Architect. Whatever the case, Davud Ağa's death in 1007/ 1599–1600 was probably by violence, and the sticky end to which his successor as Court Architect, Dalgıç Ahmed, also came must reflect the formidable intrigues and resentments to which, in the frequent changes of Grand Vizier from the 1580s onwards, the appointment had become subject.

During Davud Ağa's tenure of office architectural activity in Istanbul remained at a high level: there was significant progress on the Yeni Cami on the Golden Horn (though it remained unfinished till 1663); the mosques of Cerrâhpaşa, Nişancı Mehmed Pasha, and Mesih Pasha were all completed; and in addition a grand Imperial pavilion, the Yalı Köşk on the Seraglio point, and various hammams and mausolea were built. This suggests that under Sinan the organization of the office had become thoroughly stabilized, with enough executive capacity for an outsider of limited experience to run it efficiently. Henceforth it was to come under the *Şehremin*, the head of the Bîrûn who was responsible for the finance of public building in Istanbul. He headed a committee that included the Inspector of Waterworks, the Commander of the Acemioğlans in Istanbul, the Intendant of the State builder's yard and the Surveyor of Repairs, the Court Architect and his Deputy, and a secretariat and a number of specialized master craftsmen (*kalfa*).

Among Sinan's immediate successors as Court Architect Dalgıç Ahmed was conspicuous in having become a Pasha. He began his career as a Çavuş and first appears in an architectural context in 999/1590–1 in connection with works under the supervision of the Grand Vizier, Sinan Pasha, on the Yalı Köşk at the Seraglio Point, with responsibility for bulk purchases of timber and lead. In 1004/1595–6 he was made Inspector of Waterworks, retaining this position up to the death in Safer 1007/September 1598 of the Court Architect Davud Ağa, whom he succeeded. He was responsible for miscellaneous repairs and maintenance on the Old and New Palaces, and on two of the principal schools for pages, the Galata Saray and the palace of Ibrahim Pasha. His most important project, however, was the mausoleum of Mehmed III at Hagia Sophia completed in 1008/1599–1600, for which he also executed a domed octagonal Qur'an chest inlaid with ivory, mother-of-pearl, and tortoiseshell. In a register dated April 1606 he is listed as 'sometime Court Architect', his place evidently having been taken by Mehmed Ağa, the architect of the mosque of Sultan Ahmed I. This followed upon his advancement to the Pashalık and his appointment as governor of the fortress of Silistre on the Danube (Silistra in Bulgaria). Less than a year later, however, he was killed in a skirmish near Mihalıç near Bursa.

Mehmed Ağa inspired a treatise on architecture, the *Risâle-i Mi'mâriye* by Cafer Efendi, who, however, rather negligently fails to give a list of his buildings. He was brought from European Turkey (possibly from Elbasani in Albania) as a *devşirme* boy in 970/1562–3 and served for five years as an Acemioğlan, passing out into the Bostancıs: his first salaried appointment was as gardener at the tomb of Süleyman the Magnificent. The following year he was appointed to the staff of the Imperial gardens. Like

Davud Ağa and Dalgıç Ahmed he also worked under Sinan at
Edirne. His first appointment as architect was evidently in 1586
to supervise the completion of the works on the mosque of Murad
III at Manisa (p. 34).

A mission to Egypt (in 999/1590–1 or the following year) was
followed by travels in Syria and Palestine, and by a much longer
tour all over the Balkans, Central and Eastern Europe, and the
Crimea, gathering intelligence and inspecting fortresses. In 1002/
1591–2 he was Hüsrev Pasha's lieutenant on his appointment
as governor of Diyarbekir and then as Commander-in-Chief of
Syria, when he was appointed local governor in the Hauran.
In 1005 or 1006/1596–7 or 1597–8 he returned to Istanbul and
on Davud Ağa's death the following year, when he was probably
appointed Inspector of Waterworks, he worked on various projects
of his successor, Dalgıç Ahmed, and was promoted to Court
Architect in October 1606. The most important of the buildings
he planned or supervised was the mosque of Ahmed I on the
Hippodrome, the Blue Mosque (begun 1018/1609–10, but still
unfinished in 1023/1614–5, when Cafer Efendi's treatise ends).

Cafer Efendi gives considerable importance to Mehmed Ağa's
skill in inlay work, to which he owed two major promotions.
Among his works, some of them still extant, were a mother-
of pearl lectern (rahle) presented to Murad III in 998/1589–90,
which earned him promotion to Kapıcı, and a Qur'an chest dated
1025/1616 [Fig. 5], for the tomb of Ahmed I. Cafer Efendi ascribes
this accomplishment to Sinan's tuition and Mehmed Ağa's
architectural skill to the geometry it taught him—though there
is no evidence that Sinan practised this himself. Was it just chance,
then, that two successive Court Architects practised the craft, as
a hobby as it were, or that two workers in mother-of pearl practised
architecture? Hardly, for late sixteenth- and early seventeenth-
century Ottoman Qur'an-chests almost all have striking
architectural forms, with domes on transitional zones surmounting
them, and the visual relation is apparent inside as well as out.
They were thus by-products of architectural models (which need
not, of course, have been structurally accurate) built for presentation

Fig. 5. Koran chest inlaid with ebony, ivory, and mother-of-pearl, probably the work of Mehmed Ağa (1025/1616) for the tomb of Sultan Ahmed I. Istanbul, Turkish and Islamic Art Museum 6.

to the Sultan, to give him some idea of the elevation of the building he had commanded. In that respect they are the counterpart of the elevation of Süleymaniye depicted, for example, in the *Sûrnâme* of Intizâmî (TKS H. 1344 191a, *c*.1582) [Fig. 6]: the ability to make fine models was an accomplishment highly appropriate to a Court architect, and it is scarcely surprising, therefore, that Dalgıç Ahmed and Mehmed Ağa should both have been distinguished for it.

The contrast is very marked between Sinan and his three successors in terms of the buildings attributed to them. But they were very probably middle-aged by the time they came to be appointed and they held their positions for a very much shorter time. Nor is their output a matter for criticism: the productivity of a Court Architect depended upon his patrons and their willingness to spend money. Their careers are in any case an interesting indication of the accomplishments thought necessary for a Court Architect—though one should not discount the possibility that some of their earlier appointments were irrelevant, or blind alleys.

The organization of the Court Architect's office in Istanbul was paralleled by that of the Campaign Architects (*Sefer Mi'mârları*, usually attached to the Sipahis) who worked as siege engineers as well as on the construction and maintenance of fortresses. Although Sinan at least once was ordered to draft workmen from his force for campaign duties there is little evidence that either they or the Campaign Architects remained under his control.

Makka and Madina were also a special case. By Selim I's conquest of the Hijaz in 1517 the Ottomans gained control of the Holy Places of Islam, the two Harams at Makka and Madina, appropriating from the Mamluks of Syria and Egypt the prized title of Guardian of the Holy Places (Arabic, *Khadim al-Haramayn al-Sharifayn*). They were far away and difficult to reach and the modest Ottoman military presence there demanded considerable finesse in dealing with a population that received substantial subventions from pious foundations for their benefit. The later sixteenth-century historian Mustafa Âlî cynically observed that the principal motive of those who endowed pious foundations

Fig. 6. *Masons in procession, bearing an elevation of the mosque of Süleymaniye in 1582 before Sultan Murad III. Sûrnâme of Intizâmî (c. 1582). Istanbul, Topkapı Saray Library H. 1344, folio 192ᵇ–193ᵃ (detail).*

there was to show off. However, in the Hijaz the two motives went hand in hand: to provide for the manifold needs of the vast temporary influxes of pilgrims, particularly for water, food, and lodging; and to demonstrate the Sultans' piety by the lavishness of their buildings, or their restorations, and their endowments. It is notable, for example, that at Makka and Madina the Ottomans, who generally avoided such ostentation in the great buildings of Istanbul, did not stint the use of gold and silver in the decoration of architecture.

Makka and Madina had their own Inspector of Waterworks, who was granted not a fief but a yearly salary. Works were financed partly from the revenues of Egypt and partly by the central authorities. In 1571, for example, 60,000 gold pieces were sent from Istanbul to Sinan Pasha, Commander-in Chief of Egypt for works at Makka. Nevertheless financing was often inadequate and the Inspector of Waterworks had his work cut out to ensure a proper supply. In 1585 there was even a complaint to the Sultan's Council (*Dîvân-ı Hümâyûn*) in Istanbul that an aqueduct built by Süleyman the Magnificent at Makka had not functioned for twenty years, even though the staff appointed to oversee it had not failed to collect their salaries!

The problems were not limited, however, to the provisioning and accommodation of pilgrims (which were, in any case, partly financed by monetary benefactions). The only building material locally available was stone: timber, iron, lead, bricks, mortar and nails, and even tools and implements, had all to be imported; and coordination to ensure punctual delivery was excessively difficult. Even when orders were perfectly clear, moreover, they were not always fulfilled to the letter. There was a perennial shortage of skilled labour, which had to be drafted, often unwillingly, from Syria or Egypt. The cost of buildings and repairs was consequently high. And even when building projects were fully realized they might fail to work because the Hijaz was a backwater in the Ottoman career structure. Of the four *medreses* endowed by Süleyman the Magnificent at Makka the Hanbali *medrese* failed to find a professor (*müderris*), in spite of special inducements to candidates from

Istanbul, and had to be turned into a School of Tradition (*Dârü'l-Hadîs*); and in later years there are frequent complaints that, for want of teaching staff or pupils, these foundations were often misused as residences for affluent pilgrims. Only an architect on the spot with full responsibilities and unlimited powers could have achieved even moderate efficiency, and that explains why, except in very serious cases, the Court Architect in Istanbul was so rarely involved.

Under Süleyman the Magnificent and his immediate successors, major works at the two Harams took place, though sometimes in spite of opposition from local Hijaz notables and the Sharifs of Makka. In 931/1524–5 Süleyman replaced two of the six minarets of the Haram at Makka, one built by the Abbasid Caliph al-Mansur (reigned 136–58/754–75) and another built by the Caliph al-Hadi (reigned 159–70/775–85), adding a seventh, the tallest, towards the end of his reign. He also endowed a soup kitchen (*imaret*) in memory of his wife, Hürrem. Most important, he began the substantial rebuilding of the arcades that surrounded the Ka'ba on all four sides. This continued under Selim II, when a shortage of timber caused by the rebuilding of the Ottoman fleet following its destruction at Lepanto (1571) delayed works considerably, and an architect, Mehmed Çavuş, was dispatched from Istanbul to oversee their completion[9]: previously he had been sent from Istanbul to supervise works on the mausoleum of Şehzade Mustafa at Bursa. By the time he arrived 34 of the 150 domes of the arcades had been rebuilt.[10] Controversy nevertheless occurred: the cobbling of the arcades cut and bruised the knees of those pilgrims without prayer-carpets as they made their prostrations, and the authorities decided to repave the whole courtyard with marble. That caused objections, perhaps on grounds of ostentation, but after consultations between the Ottoman authorities and the local notables the repaving was completed in 1576.

[9]BBA *MD 15*, p. 182 no.1531, 28 Cemâziyül'ahir 979/17 Oct. 1571.
[10]BBA *MD 22*, p. 296 no. 587; p. 313 no. 624, both dated 981/1573–4.

It was doubtless for lack of qualified personnel on the spot that towards the end of Sinan's life non-architects were appointed in charge of works at Makka and Madina. In 1585, perhaps as a direct result of Sinan's pilgrimage to the Holy Places the previous year, a Chief Painter (*nakkaşbaşı*), Lutfullah, who is described, nevertheless, as experienced in the maintenance of buildings, was appointed Clerk of the Works (*mu'temed*) at the tomb of the Prophet at Madina.[11] The problems at Makka, however, continued. The topography of the Haram there left it constantly vulnerable to flash floods, which the construction of dams and protective earthworks was unable to prevent. Because in the view of the clerisy the Ka'ba was divinely created and repairs to it had been undertaken by the prophets, major repairs and alterations under the Abbasids and then under the Mamluks had been kept to a minimum. Sinan (evidently in 1584 while making the Pilgrimage) had inspected it and found it in a structurally dangerous state, the golden gutter (*Altın Oluk*, Arabic *Mizab al-Rahma*), which was meant to channel rainwater from the roof, having lost most of its gold and the roof being rotten. However, what with Sinan's advanced age and the Persian and Hungarian campaigns of the 1580s and 1590s, nothing was done. In 1019/1610–11 Sun'ullah Efendi, a former Şeyhülislâm, made the Pilgrimage, registered that the building was in a worse state than ever and on his return convinced Ahmed I that repairs were urgent. Exceptionally, the Court Architect, Mehmed Ağa, was brought in from Istanbul to oversee the restorations. He verified the dimensions of the roof-beams in the Palace archives, made new designs for beams and braces, and supervised the manufacture of the golden casing for the gutter, as well as of three gold locks for the tomb of the Prophet at Madina, and an outdoor pulpit (*minbar*) for the Maqam Ibrahim in the Haram at Makka. To ensure that the braces would fit measured drawings had been made, but to make things doubly sure they were dispatched with a gang of artisans from Istanbul so that nothing could go wrong.

[11]BBA *MD* 60, p. 25 no. 58–9, 993/1585, dated 28 Şevval 993/21 Oct. 1585.

3

Sinan's status

The fact that Sinan and his colleagues figure rather rarely in the collections of Court edicts could be taken as evidence that for the most part their work gave satisfaction: administrative orders are normally issued only when things go wrong. A significant exception was the mosque of Muradiye at Manisa, and what happened is well enough documented in the Mühimme registers[1] to throw important light on how Sinan's office worked. A mosque completed in 979/1571–2 under the supervision of the local architect at Manisa, of which Şehzade Murad (who inherited the throne as Murad III in 1574) was currently governor, turned out to be too small. In 990/1582–3 permission was sought from him to enlarge it, and adjacent property, occupied by tenements belonging to another foundation, were acquired. Orders to proceed, under the supervision of a local architect, were given and the sum of 600,000 akçe was promptly sent from Istanbul. The orders were, however, misunderstood (or disobeyed): the building was largely demolished and when rebuilt was even smaller than the one it had replaced. Why, Murad III angrily demanded, could the architect not build a noble mosque like that of Kılıç Ali Pasha in Istanbul (pp. 58–60)? Sinan was then ordered to provide a plan or an elevation (kâmâme) and an architect from his office, Mahmud, was

[1] Cf. Anhegger, 1955–7.

dispatched, together with cash to the value of 10,000 gold coins, to Manisa to execute it. One of the Court Painters, Mehmed Halife, was also sent with a staff of twelve to decorate the mosque and, presumably, mount its rich Iznik tilework. Two years later, however, the dome was still unfinished: why was this? Not only had a great deal of money been spent; the area was teeming with skilled craftsmen and timber was abundant and cheap. Meanwhile Mahmud, from the Court Architect's office who was supervising the project, died. A replacement from Sinan's office, Mehmed, was appointed at 30 akçe a day in January 1586, and the mosque was finally inaugurated in December of that year, though work continued at the complex till at least 1590.

Sinan was doubtless not brought in earlier, partly because of his heavy involvement with Imperial foundations in Istanbul and at Edirne throughout the 1570s, and partly because, to begin with, the authorities—perhaps typically—assumed that a local architect could bring the project to completion. Sinan's intervention may have been ineffective because of his absence on the Pilgrimage, but the delay scarcely reflects credit on his colleague, Mahmud. Like the Ottoman authorities, we may find such slow progress on an Imperial foundation, at the residence of a Şehzade, moreover, inexplicable, but the fact that it caused so much fuss is a good indication that during Sinan's tenure of office their patience was not often strained.

The demolition may, of course, have been an accident, for the enlargement of standing buildings was always risky. That of Sinan's Atik Valide mosque at Toptaşı above Üsküdar with side ranges carried out a year and a half after the dome was completed (early in 1582) must have called on all Sinan's reserves of experience, for it involved demolishing two of the walls supporting the dome, gambling on the calculation that they were structurally unimportant.

Sinan and his staff also belonged to the privileged group of Ottoman officials who received a monthly salary (often paid, however, between two and nine months in arrears), the Müşâherehorân. In Palace registers of the 1550s they were largely composed of financial officials, secretaries, and high officers, including the heads of some Janissary corps such as the Şahinciyan (Falconers).

In addition to the annual revenue from his *arpalık*, by the early 1550s Sinan as Court Architect was receiving 65 akçe a day/1814 akçe a month. His permanent staff received considerably less:[2] Hidâyet, who evidently had special responsibilities at Edirne, received 23 akçe a day; Kâsım Mermeri, with special responsibilities for marble work, 8–10 akçe a day; Hacı Mustafa, 10 akçe a day; Ali 10 akçe a day; Bâkî, a *sipahi* or cavalryman, 24 akçe a day; Hüseyin, another *sipahi*, 21 akçe a day; Yorgi, 8 akçe a day; Simo, with the odd sobriquet Tâcir (merchant), 10 akçe a day; Mehmed b. Mustafa, 10 akçe a day; and Sefer b. Ahmed, 7 akçe a day. To judge from his much larger salary, 33 akçe a day, Sinan's deputy at the time was a certain Emre, though nothing is known of his works and he later disappears from the registers. These daily salaries were evidently basic pay and extra duties entitled his staff to regular supplements. As Court Architect Sinan also qualified for seasonal gratuities. His winter 'uniform allowance' (*âdet-i zemestânî*), for example, was 3000 akçe cash and a robe of mohair trimmed or lined with sable.

Though, by virtue of his appointment, Sinan belonged to the feudal military class (*askerî*), the grant of land that went with it was modest. Nor does he seem to have cared greatly for financial advancement. Whereas the registers of military appointments in the Istanbul archives record numerous efforts by his colleagues in the Palace, like the Chief Court Painter (*nakkaşbaşı*), to gain fiefs for their staffs, Sinan and his officials are conspicuous by their absence, which suggests that he was neither a careerist himself nor an empire builder on their behalf. Given his modest remuneration the endowments of the *vakfs* he founded amounting to 300,000 akçe cash, together with land and windmills, bringing in a total annual revenue of 42,265 akçe make an impressive sum. The foundations were mostly in Istanbul (a small mosque,

[2]BBA D.BRZ 7 and D.BZM 20617, both dated 3 Muharrem 961–27 Zilka'de 962/19 Dec. 1553–23 Oct. 1555.

two Qur'an schools (*mektebs*) and a fountain), but also included fountains (*çeşmes*) at his birthplace Ağırnas in the province of Kayseri[3] and at villages in the districts of Haslar (i.e. Istanbul *extra muros* on the Thracian side) and Vize, where his *arpalık* was situated. Whether he supervised their construction we do not know.

If most of what we can say about Sinan as a practising architect has to be deduced from his buildings, how can we be certain which they were? Of course, some of the discrepancies in the written sources are the result of a copyist's misreadings; some are sheer mistakes; and since the three lists are not entirely independent of one another the appearance of a building in all three may not be conclusive. On the other hand, Sinan is unlikely to have had anything to do with buildings that appear in none of the sources. Of the 314 buildings in all three accounts, 52 have been substantially rebuilt, 32 are untraceable and 25 are ruined: the best-represented surviving buildings are bridges, aqueducts, and hospitals, followed by mosques, tombs, and hospitals. Of these 73 per cent are in the environs of Istanbul, which shows that his architectural practice was very largely metropolitan. The total of two hundred or so recognizably sixteenth-century buildings is still impressive, even for an architect as long-lived as Sinan. But even if we accept much more conservative estimates, as compared to other Islamic architects or, indeed, to his contemporaries in Renaissance Europe, his achievement is extraordinary.

The discrepancies in contemporary lists of Sinan's buildings and modern authors' very different estimates of their reliability, may be less perplexing than at first sight appears. An obvious explanation is that the degree of his involvement must often have been very unclear and that not all of his biographers, or even Sinan himself, took the same view. As Court Architect, he was head of a sizeable office, large enough to continue to work efficiently when various members of it were called up on military service, so that quite a few of the projects credited to

[3]BBA *MD 12*, p.157 no. 338, 24 Zilka'de 978/30 Apr. 1571.

him must have been the work of his staff. Thus in 1560[4] he is ordered to send an architect, Celâleddin, of whom otherwise nothing is recorded, to build the complex, consisting of a mosque, an *imaret*, a caravansaray, and a *hamam* (bath), at Karapınar near Konya founded by Prince Selim (later Selim II) and dated by a chronogram 971/1563–4; and an order of the same year[5] appoints Todoros, who had completed Süleyman the Magnificent's complex in Damascus, to the Court Architect's office. Notwithstanding, these two buildings are ascribed in all three lists of Sinan's works to Sinan himself. Karapınar lay on the Konya–Adana road, so the caravansaray, now ruined, may well have been intended as the principal element of the foundation. Kuran suggests therefore that the complex was designed by Sinan in Istanbul and that he personally instructed Celâleddin, who must have been one of the architects in his office and a man, therefore, of proven ability, to direct and execute the project on the spot.

Since Sinan's responsibilities were primarily to the Sultan or the Imperial family it was necessary for him to delegate many of the projects with which he was associated; and indeed, his name appears relatively infrequently in the archives in connection with specific building works. Many of these posed relatively minor problems of structure, landscaping, or even design and could, therefore, once plans had been drawn up, have been left completely for his subordinates to execute. Even they would not necessarily have been overworked, for Ottoman building was considerably facilitated by specialization in the workforce—in the construction of minarets, domes, etc. as well as in building materials and even architectural decoration. Their major responsibility would thus, like Sinan's, have been supervision and coordination.

How did Sinan learn his craft? The diversity of his buildings and the constant need for special solutions made standardization difficult. On various occasions he received orders to draw up

[4]BBA *MD* 3, p. 374 nos.1106–8, 18 Şaban 967/15 May 1560.
[5]BBA *MD* 4, p. 87 no.198, 23 Ramazan 967/18 Jun. 1560.

FIG. 7. Istanbul, the mosque of Süleymaniye. From Seyyid Lokman, Süleymânnâme, copied in 987/1579. Dublin, Chester Beatty Library MS 413, folio 119ᵃ.

a *kârnâme* for a building, though in different contexts this could mean a plan, an elevation, a model, or even detailed estimates of labour and materials. Remains of plans in the Ottoman archives suggest that these were often little more than sketches, which took no account either of the site or the contours or the sight-lines, and which, not being to scale, give no idea of of a building's actual size, weight, or mass. For each plan, moreover, the corresponding elevation had to be worked out and the quantities and costs of the necessary materials calculated. It is scarcely conceivable that Sinan, or his fellow architects, could have learned the essential elements of structure from merely looking at buildings. As Mainstone suggests, to judge from the building histories of St Peter's in Rome or St Paul's in London, his major works must necessarily have involved considerable testing of alternatives, perhaps on paper, both for the spatial planning of the interior, including the vaulting, and the structure necessary to realize it, not to speak of harmonizing the visual character of interior and exterior. The model or elevation of Süleymaniye, known from depictions in illustrated chronicles like the *Sûrnâme* of Intizâmî and the Chester Beatty Süleymânnâme [Figs. 6–7], carried by the architects parading before Murad III, must therefore derive from his practice.

Responsibility for calculating the quantities of materials required was not the least of the Court Architect's worries. Labour relations could also be tricky. An order fixing wages for carpenters employed on Imperial works[6] complains that they have been moonlighting for higher wages: if that continues culprits are to be apprehended and punished. That was not the end of the matter. Subsequent orders to Sinan[7] then allege that although builders, carpenters, and masons have been given a substantial raise, those working on the mosque of Nişancı Mehmed Pasha in Istanbul are refusing to work for even that. We do not have the grounds

[6]BBA *MD* 58, p. 83 no. 257, 17 Cemaziyül'evvel 993/17 May 1585.
[7]BBA *MD* 62, p. 55 no.127, 16 Cemaziyül'evvel 995/14 Apr. 1587.

Fig. 8. Istanbul, Hagia Sophia. Interior.

for the workmen's case, but it suggests that the Court Architect's office may have had to contend with strikes.

HAGIA SOPHIA

What Sinan or Mustafa Sâ'î thought to be a good, or a great, building is often difficult to tell. The Ottoman descriptive vocabulary of architecture is largely hyperbolical and its structural significance difficult to evaluate. However, the first volume of the later seventeenth-century traveller Evliyâ Çelebi's monumental *Seyâhatnâme* (Book of Travels)—which is devoted to Istanbul and its buildings—makes it clear that before him Sinan had one of the greatest architectural topoi of all, Justinian's great church, Hagia Sophia. This had accumulated a rich body of Islamic legend, combining Muslim notices of Constantinople with a substantial body of late Byzantine texts, often known as the *Patria*. Translated into Turkish as early as 1479, it went through Persian as well many further Turkish versions. The Ottoman versions often embroider so grotesquely on what was—even to begin with—a somewhat credulous account that they must, from one point of view, be considered as an early form of science fiction. Their popularity, which lasted at least till the late sixteenth century, nevertheless shows how central Hagia Sophia was to Ottoman architectural thought (see Fig. 8). Nothing like them is known for any Ottoman building in Istanbul, and perhaps only the traditions regarding the seventh-century Dome of the Rock in Jerusalem can approach them anywhere else in Islam.

Principally important are the associations of Hagia Sophia with Solomon's temple in Jerusalem. (According to some sources, Justinian boasted on entering Hagia Sophia in 537 AD, 'Solomon, I have outdone thee!') Not only was Hadrian's temple at Cyzicus (Ottoman Edincik), on the south coast of the Sea of Marmara, one of the great monuments of classical antiquity, which Justinian had pillaged for marbles for Hagia Sophia and which was subsequently pillaged for Süleymaniye, held to be a palace built for Solomon; Hagia Sophia was also believed to have been built over one of the dungeons that Solomon had built to confine his rebellious jinns (doubtless a garbled explanation of the vast columned underground cisterns in the centre of the Byzantine city).

Byzantine architectural genius was also canonized in Ottoman eyes by the first of the legendary founders of Byzantium (the other two, more realistically, were Byzas and Constantine), Yanko b. Madyan (an ingenious corruption of *Nikomedia*, now Izmid/Izmit on the north-eastern shore of the Marmara, which later Christian sources had mistakenly identified with Constantine's original capital), whose descent they traced to the legendary pre-Islamic architects of Arabia, the Kings of 'Ad in the Yemen. In the early sixteenth century what passed for the remains of the temple 'Yanko' built were still being shown on the Hippodrome on the site of the future palace of Ibrahim Pasha. Not that any of these legends had any effect on Sinan's practice, any more than the legendary *De Mirabilibus Urbis Romae* affected late-medieval or Renaissance builders in Rome; but they certainly encouraged his patrons in what to expect in the way of awe-inspiring grandiosity.

To Süleyman the Magnificent, the Solomon of his time, these legends were especially potent and suggest that he intended Sinan's first major project in Istanbul, the Şehzade complex [Fig. 20], to be a recreation of Solomon's Temple, and outdo Justinian too. Although in the view of Celâlzâde Mustafa and other historians it was built in memory of Şehzade Mehmed (d. 4 October 1543), Süleyman's favourite son and intended heir, Sâ'î tells us that works began in June 1543, before Mehmed's unexpected death. The lapse of time between an Ottoman Sultan's decision to build and the start of works is extremely difficult to estimate precisely, but, with larger buildings at least, the preliminary preparation was considerable. Hence the Şehzade project, a first Süleymaniye, must have been ordered well before that, probably as a pious gesture at the outset of Süleyman's 1542 Hungarian campaign. Its dedication to Mehmed's memory was therefore most probably an afterthought.

By 1547, with Habsburg Austria—his principal adversary in Europe—humiliated by the payment of tribute and with the Şehzade project still a year away from completion, Süleyman evidently changed his mind. Now only a second, grander Süleymaniye, which could directly challenge the great mass of Hagia Sophia, would adequately reflect his Solomonic glory. The foundation stone of the *mihrab* of Süleymaniye, the beginning of building works, was laid by his Şeyhülislâm Ebüssuûd in June 1550 but, given Süleyman's absence on campaign in Iran from early 1548 to late 1549, the Süleymaniye project, with the major preliminary works it entailed, must have been approved no later than the beginning of 1548. In fact, of all Sinan's works it is closest in plan and basic structure to Hagia Sophia, though the treatment of the interior space is markedly different. Significantly, the best view of it is from Galata, where the non-Muslim population of the Ottoman capital was concentrated, as Melchior Lorichs's panorama of 1557, drawn only months before its inauguration in October of that year, clearly demonstrates (see Fig. 1). Its only competitor on the Istanbul skyline is Hagia Sophia which, however, because of its mass and more impressive situation, it markedly outdoes. This can be no accident: its message was as much to the Europeans and 'unbelievers' in Galata as to the pious Muslim population of Istanbul.

Sinan must have learned from other Byzantine buildings in Istanbul, notably another great foundation of Justinian's, the church of Saints Sergius and Bacchus (Küçük Ayasofya) at Kadırga, begun in 527 AD. But it was scarcely coincidence that in the decade following the inauguration of Süleymaniye yet further Turkish versions of the legends concerning the foundation of Hagia Sophia were dedicated to Süleyman. These accentuate the Solomonic elements, the former even claiming that Solomon was the original builder not merely of the temple at Cyzicus but also of the Topkapı Saray.

The study of Hagia Sophia was to stand Sinan in good stead. Its lavish endowments were doubtless adequate for running repairs, but there appear to have been no major repairs to the fabric since it suffered damage in the serious earthquake of 1509. Sinan's works at Hagia Sophia in 1573 under Selim II and which continued under Murad III, his successor, were regarded by Ottoman historians like Selânikî Mustafa as the most important architectural achievement of his reign—rightly so, since without a thorough grasp of its structure repairs would have been useless or, worse, could have aggravated the damage. The orders[8] were issued in response to complaints of encroachments on its walls and sanctuary: a certain Ibrahim had sunk a well inside and built a two–storey latrine, as well as two arcades, one with another latrine and the other with rooms and a kitchen. These must be removed. The Sultan then inspected the building with a committee of experts, including Sinan and the Şeyhülislâm who gave a *fetva* that all the surrounding buildings, including the Imperial storehouse for building materials, must be demolished, leaving a space of thirty-five cubits to right and left of the mosque. The minaret over the half-dome (*sic*) was to be demolished and replaced by one built on the buttress in front of it. In the area freed by demolition drains were to be laid. The lead for the roofing was to be restored and the stone and brick from the demolitions reused in the repairs. Those who had opposed the Sultan's orders on the grounds that Hagia Sophia need not be preserved since it was built by non-Muslims deserved to be executed as infidels. As Emerson and Van Nice have observed, it was, of course, impossible that the thin shell of a semidome could support a minaret of any kind. That referred to was the original south turret of the church that in the reign of Mehmed II was heightened and transformed into the first minaret.

The most conspicuous of Sinan's additions are the two minarets built after Selim II's death at the south-west and north-west corners, originally planned as three–balconied and with three concentric interior staircases but prudently revised and simplified. These, with the two minarets on the *qibla* side already existing, brought Hagia Sophia in exterior visual appearance closer to Sinan's splendid mosque, Selimiye, built for Selim II at Edirne [Fig. 9, Fig. 10]. It is possible that they incidentally helped to offset the progressive deformations caused by the outwards thrust

[8]BBA *MD* 22, p. 82 no.171, 20 Şa'ban 981/21 Jun. 1573.

Fig. 9. Edirne, Mosque of Selim II (982/1574–5).

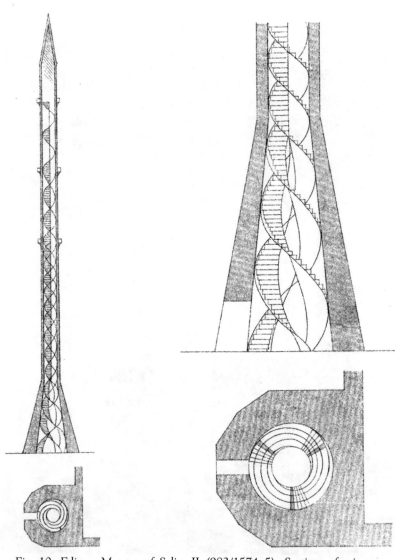

Fig. 10. Edirne, Mosque of Selim II (982/1574–5). Sections of minaret, showing triple staircase. After F. von Hochstetter, 'Die Moschee Sultan Selim's II. in Adrianopel', Allegemeine Bauzeitung 35 (1870), fig. 194.

of the higher vaults. Otherwise buttresses were strengthened by inserting iron tie-rods and renewing the barrel vaults connecting them to the walls; the north-south penetrations of the main piers at gallery level were filled in; and some of the windows of the tympana were narrowed and four of the dome windows blocked up. These major repairs were followed by orders to build a pair of *medreses* in the name of Selim II on to Hagia Sophia and to clear space for a tomb there. Because of Selim's death the following year, however, they were not in fact built, but the tomb was completed under his successor, Murad III, in 985/1577: his tomb was built next to it.

4

Sinan's architectural development

The idea of complex pious foundations with a mosque as their centre had a long past in Islam. But the Ottomans certainly developed the idea, with an ever-greater variety of components, generously planned and often with significant spatial interrelations, even if they were not necessarily enclosed within a single boundary wall. Practically all Sinan's buildings (with the exception of palaces and pavilions) were complexes and to that extent traditional. To agree, moreover, that Sinan represented the acme of the Ottoman classical style is not to imply that he alone created it. Indeed, it is characteristic of any classical style that it evolves, if at all, only slowly: patrons who are generally conservative in their tastes tend to be even more conservative when they are faced with ready-made classical standards. A brief survey of some of the major monuments of fifteenth- and early sixteenth-century Edirne and Istanbul shows that the major innovations upon which Sinan developed date back a hundred years before his appointment as Court Architect in 1537, in particular, to one of the most innovative of earlier Ottoman buildings, the Üç Şerefeli Mosque at Edirne (841–51/1437–57) built by Murad II. This itself crystallizes a number of tendencies in Ottoman architecture of the Emirate period, when the Ottomans were merely one of a series of principalities struggling for supremacy. Its plan is probably more traditional than it looks, with a central domed area flanked by structures with separate entrances. To this, however, it adds a rather shallow elongated courtyard, larger than the mosque itself, with an ornamental fountain (*şadırvan*). The central domed hexagon, (24 metres in diameter) the largest Ottoman dome to date, towers above the side wings and is stoutly built with two great hexagonal piers and conspicuous tie-beams for all the arches. It also has four minarets, the tallest with three balconies (which give the mosque its name) at the north-west corner.

Mehmed II's great complex in Istanbul, Fâtih, included a hospital and a substantial library among its elements, and in addition eight *medreses*, flanking his mosque in groups of four on a great raised esplanade. It was, however, so badly damaged in an earthquake in 1766 that the mosque and many of the other buildings had to be rebuilt. The courtyard of the mosque was very nearly equal in area to the mosque itself, which lacks, however, the lateral elements of the Üç Şerefeli mosque and which established two minarets, rather than four, as standard for Imperial foundations. Too little survives of the original fabric, however, for it to be a reliable document for the evolution of Imperial taste.

That, however, may be deduced from the foundations of his successor, Bayazid II (1481–1512), both at Edirne and in Istanbul. The former (completed 895/1489–90) consists of three major blocks, enclosed within a spacious walled enceinte: a hospital, a madhouse, and a medical school; an imaret or refectory, storehouse, and bakery; and, at the centre, a mosque. The mosque, with a dome a little more than 20 metres in diameter, is fronted by a broad courtyard, half the width of its domed portico, and has nine-domed lateral constructions extending beyond the portico, so that they can be entered from outside the courtyard, or from the mosque, as well as from the courtyard itself. Its two minarets are placed at the corners of the side buildings, their style foreshadowing the minarets of Istanbul, being polygonal on polygonal panelled bases, with markedly taller and slenderer shafts and only a single balcony. The lateral constructions have given rise to much discussion, since they are not spatially part of the mosque. The entrances from outside may suggest that they were, as some scholars have argued, hospices for travellers, or possibly temporary abodes for Sufis, though they could also have been for the staff of the mosque—the imam, müezzins, etc. Whatever their function, however, it is interesting that the mosque of Fâtih did not have them, and their last Imperial appearance is at Selimiye in Istanbul (completed 929/1522), which derives in many respects from the plan of Bayazid II's Edirne mosque. Sinan in many of his mosques often found it convenient to extend the domed space laterally, but without breaking up the space, so that barely a reminiscence of these features survives.

In materials these buildings also document the Ottoman sultans' established taste for rich marbles, which they shared not only with their Byzantine predecessors but their European maritime rivals, the Venetians and the Genoese who, like them, pillaged the Classical sites of the Eastern Mediterranean. In the Ottoman case this included marble from the Marmara quarries (the ancient Proconessos), which had exported marble all over the Mediterranean in antiquity but which do not seem to have been worked between the death of Justinian and the mid- or later sixteenth century, and the splendour of their architecture is a testimony to their single-minded acquisition of ancient materials, which they stored for security in the Imperial storehouse, for issue as required. The organization of these marble hunts was to reach its climax under Sinan.

Bayazid II's complex in Istanbul (inaugurated 1505) was generously planned, with its elements disposed at different levels round a square that fronted the mosque. Built by his Court Architect, Ya'kubşah b. Sultanşah, its unity of conception testifies to a well-manned and coordinated office. The areas of the courtyard and the interior of the mosque are virtually identical, and although lateral projections with porticoes are conceived on the exterior as separate constructions the interior space has been unified. The addition of a second semi-dome doubtless derives from Hagia Sophia, an example to Sinan is his long struggle to outdo Justinian's great church. One conspicuous feature of the building was the emphasis of the gates into the courtyard from the exterior in the form of profiled portals with grand stalactite hoods, the grandest of all being from the courtyard into the mosque. Traditionally this goes back to the earlier fifteenth-century architecture of Bursa, or even to the buildings of thirteenth-century Seljuk Anatolia, but the treatment of such entrances as façades created problems in the lay out of mosque porticoes and was to be progressively abandoned by Sinan.

These earlier Imperial foundations at Edirne and in Istanbul, in plan, elevation, and constructional technique, were a graphic example to the budding Court Architect. The marble work of Bayazid II's mosque in Istanbul, which is of exceptional refinement, also shows that a decorative canon of profiles, cornices, and friezes had been elaborated and carefully adapted in their architectural use. It remains to be demonstrated how many of its elements were taken over into Sinan's buildings, and it is improbable that he slavishly copied them, but they provided him with an admirably comprehensive vocabulary from which to work.

Generally, Sinan's works are considered as if there was no overlap from one project to another—quite unrealistically, given the imperative demands of Imperial patronage. This considerably complicates their chronology, and any overall discussion of his architectural development. Progress on one project, moreover, inevitably affected other projects in various ways, sometimes deleteriously, and may even have affected their appearance or structure. Consistency demanded that Sinan's staff thought very much as he did, which suggests that the creation of a classical style, with which Sinan is credited, was their joint achievement, possibly with himself as *primus inter pares*—though since we know even less of *them* that may sound rather speculative.

The Court Architect's basic task, to place and orient a mosque of a certain size or capacity, with all its dependencies from its atrium to the latrines, on a given site within the (financial) limitations of the endowment, and to balance elegance of layout with suitably imposing structure, admitted of many solutions. Grandeur also depended on the appropriate use of conventional materials—timber, brick, and stone—with only metal cramps and tie-beams to reinforce them. Here Sinan's preponderant use of stone, at least for his buildings in Istanbul, emphasized the contrast between public buildings and private architecture, which was mostly of wood or half-timbered (*kâgir/kârgir*, from the Persian *kâhgil*).

Kuban has, notwithstanding, observed that a persistent feature of Sinan's approach to mosque design is the central importance he gives the dome, which he viewed not as one covering among others, but as primordial, with the requirement that, as far as possible, interior space should be a unified whole. Concomitantly, the arcaded side façades of his buildings are often more elaborate than the front façade, which may be accentuated merely by a projecting portal, for the demand for a courtyard took precedence over a façade. Similarly, in contrast to the architecture of Byzantium, his fenestration was intended to bring maximum brilliance into the interior, rather than keeping the world out, as it were. This rationalization, however, is markedly more structural than theoretical. Sinan's use of capitals, stalactite and rhomboid, either inside or outside, has, however, nothing to do with the Classical orders of architecture—or any orders at all, in fact.

Sinan's restraint is the mark of sound practical common sense. The covered market (*arasta*) [Figs. 11, 12] through which the visitor approaches the mosque of Selimiye at Edirne from below was a practical solution to the visual and structural lightening of the vast retaining wall of the platform on which the mosque stands—though it may have been executed after his death, by Davud Ağa. Moreover, as at the Takiyya al-Sulaymaniyya at Damascus, a two-dimensional planning concept on a flat site with which his name is generally associated, he always produced simple solutions for buildings he had to delegate (p. 37). This is a symmetrical composition organized on flat terrain by the channel of the river Barada and enclosed by walls. The mosque and a hospice for orphans (*Dârü'l-eytâm*) face one another on the central axis, each flanked by twin caravansarays or hospices, constituting the two broken side wings. Despite later additions, *not* by Sinan, under Selim II, which somewhat detract from the effect, the scheme is still an impressive realization.

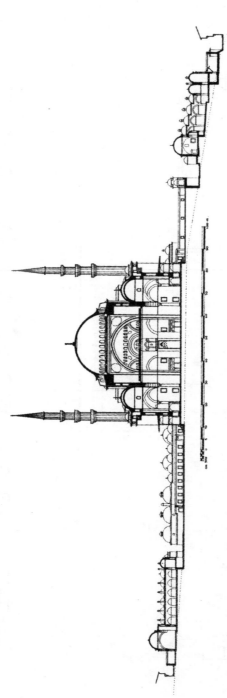

Fig. 11. Edirne, mosque of Selim II (982/1574-5). *Cross-section, showing the covered market* (arasta).

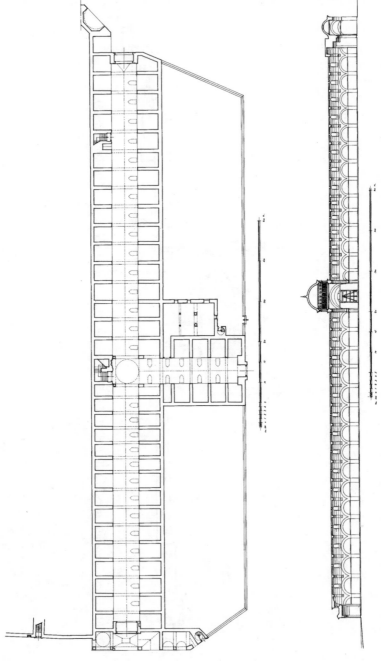

Fig. 12. Edirne. Covered market (arasta), buttressing the terrace of the mosque of Selim II. Plan and elevation.

One of the most perfect of Sinan's smaller buildings is the mosque in Istanbul he built for Esmahan Sultan, a daughter of Selim II married to his Grand Vizier, Sokollu Mehmed Pasha (which is more usually known by his name rather than hers), completed in 979/1571-2. It occupies a terrace on the steep hill behind the harbour of the district of Kadırga on the Sea of Marmara. Because of the shallowness of the terrace the courtyard, which incorporates a *medrese*, was built out on piers: its domed lecture room is built over the steep staircase up from the main entrance, which gives a dramatically foreshortened view of the fountain and the mosque behind it as one comes into the courtyard from below. Despite this masterly compression, the portico of the mosque is also impressive. The supports of the dome are expressed as exterior buttresses and remove all distraction from one's appreciation of the mosque, which fits the steep gradient of the hill behind quite extraordinarily well. The interior of the building, with low galleries on three sides, is famous for its Iznik tiles. They are concentrated on the *qibla* wall, surrounding the elegant chastely profiled marble *mihrab*, but the pendentives are also tiled; and the galleries and even the pyramidal hood of the *minbar* also have rich tilework. Because of the harmony of the designs the interior feels considerably larger and the dome considerably higher than the actual dimensions might suggest. Comparison of the plan and the section drawn to the same scale [Fig. 13, Fig. 14] shows the *medrese* floating, as it were, out from the terrace, brilliantly demonstrates the interrelations of courtyard and mosque and suggests furthermore that the height of the dome was partly determined by the decorative scheme of the *qibla* wall. It is rare in the history of architecture to find a building that expresses so well the relation of its site to its constitution, its plan, and its elevation.

Sinan's approach is also well demonstrated in two of his smaller complexes, both coincidentally at Üsküdar across the Bosphorus—one from the early part of his career, the Iskele Camii, for Süleyman's daughter, Mihrimah Sultan (954/1547-8); and the other for a Grand Vizier of Murad III, Isfendiyaroğlu Şemsi Ahmed Pasha (988/1580-1). The former is built on steeply rising ground dominating

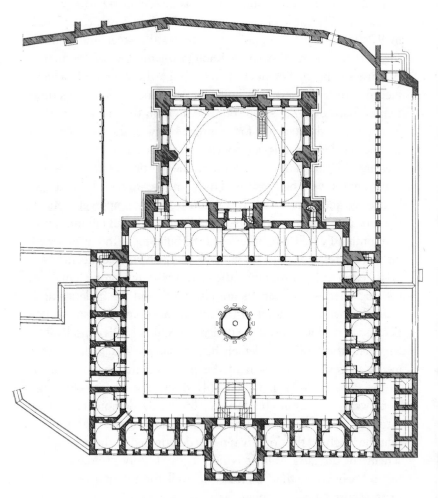

Fig. 13. Istanbul, Kadırga, Complex (külliye) of Sokollu Mehmed Pasha (979/1571–2). Plan.

the landing stage, which was the western terminus of the rich caravan trade across Anatolia and was also the assembly point for the annual Pilgrimage caravan to Makka. The mosque is set on an arcaded basement. Its massive dome is set on a heavy square base and is fronted by a double portico (a feature that Sinan was to use more than once) with a steeply pitched shed roof, into which an ornamental *şadırvan* is built. The interior is rather unsatisfactory, both the inner portico and the mosque being too dark, but the exterior, enhanced considerably by two minarets (a characteristic feature of Sultans', rather than princesses', foundations), is impressive and its ingenious use of space to fit in both a *medrese* and a *mekteb* to a difficult site is aesthetically satisfying.

The foundation of Isfendiyaroğlu Şemsi Ahmed Pasha is one of Sinan's smallest but is situated dramatically at the shore of the Bosphorus, with windows in a low wall giving views of the sea to its inmates. It consists of an L-shaped *medrese* fronted by a portico, opposite a simple domed mosque on squinches, also with an L-shaped portico, but set at 37 degrees east to it, giving the visitor a visual jolt that must surely be deliberate. The effect is reinforced by the ingenious incorporation of the minaret base into its north-west corner.

The extreme diversity of the plans of Sinan's buildings and the variety of their solutions to structural problems may suggest a constant striving towards an architectural ideal, and indeed the desire to equal or surpass the dome of Hagia Sophia seems to dominate his later years. As Gülru Necipoğlu-Kafadar has remarked, however, his alleged description of his career as a progress from apprenticeship (Şehzade) to maturity (Süleymaniye) and mastership (Selimiye at Edirne) is not only apocryphal but highly misleading. In fact, rather like Palladio's plans, his do not show any particular evolutionary pattern—for the required balance of economy, splendour, and breadth of vision and structural solidity allowed of virtually infinite solutions. Practically none of his plans are duplicates, and very few of them are copies of earlier buildings. Significantly, the only one to show clear indebtedness to the

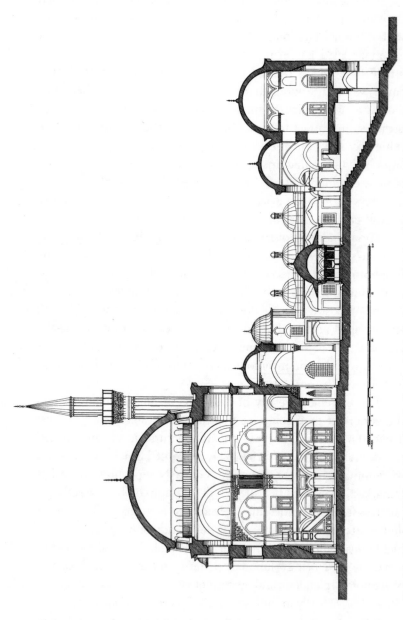

Fig. 14. Istanbul, Kadırga, Complex (külliye) of Sokollu Mehmed Pasha (979/1571–2). Section along the main axis.

plan of Hagia Sophia, that of the mosque of Kılıç Ali Pasha in Istanbul (988/1580–1), is on such a reduced scale that it could not possibly be said to challenge it as a building.

This mosque is one of three, all founded by admirals, all in areas either with naval barracks or else shipyards at the time, the other two being that of Sinan Pasha (963/1557–8), which depends on the Üç Şerefeli Mosque at Edirne, though much smaller in scale; and that of Piyale Pasha (perhaps by Sinan, 981/1573–4), which is reminiscent of Great Mosques at Bursa and at Edirne. It is unclear why three 'naval' mosques should have dictated such a conservative approach, over almost three decades. The prime need to increase usable space, in keeping with their function as places of formal prayer before the departure of the fleet, could surely have been better fulfilled by more innovative plans.

In Kuran's view the explanation of the mosque of Kılıç Ali Pasha is clear [Fig. 15, Fig. 16]. The building (completed in 988/1580–1) must have been designed following Sinan's completion of Selimiye at Edirne, hence concomitantly with the complex of Zal Mahmud Pasha at Eyüp. Its linear, directional disposition, with its interior space compartmented by rows of columns, exactly as in Hagia Sophia, runs entirely counter to the centrality of classical Ottoman architecture, which Sinan had displayed to such striking effect at Selimiye at Edirne. Despite being mentioned in all three treatises, in Kuran's view the building has been misattributed and the design is not Sinan's but must be that of a junior colleague from his office who, like Mahmud and Mehmed at Manisa, had been delegated with it under not very strict direction. This might seem plausible in view of Sinan's already advanced age—though, as we know, he was actively involved with other buildings practically up to his death—but it is open to two objections. First, its listing in all three treatises is difficult to explain away. And, secondly, it does not explain why Sinan's junior colleagues or pupils should have adopted a plan so counter to his own rules. In fact, the tension between centrality and axiality is visually exciting, and even if Kılıç Ali Pasha was to be a dead end the idea is typical of Sinan's own restless experimentation.

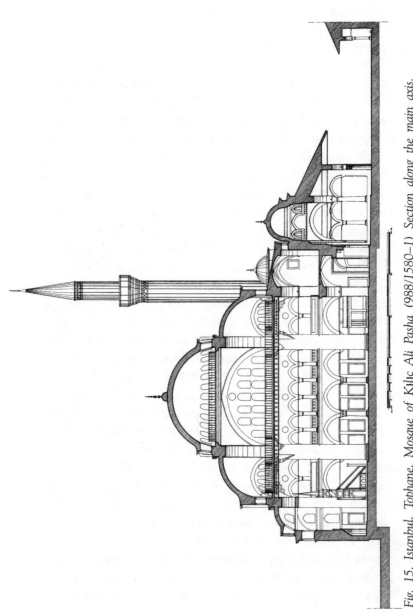

Fig. 15. Istanbul, Tophane, Mosque of Kılıç Ali Pasha (988/1580–1) Section along the main axis.

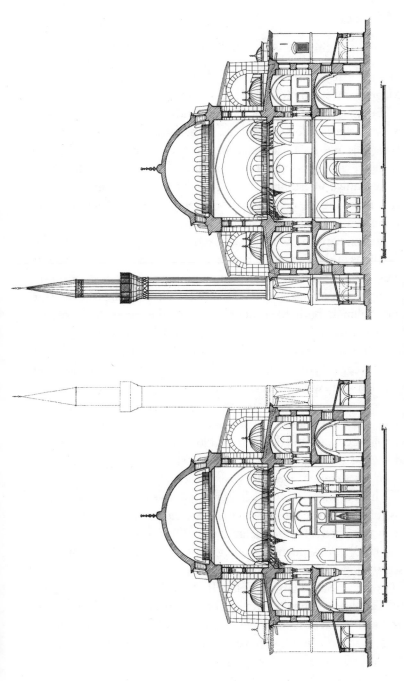

Fig. 16. Istanbul, Tophane, Mosque of Kılıç Ali Pasha (988/1580–1) Cross-sections.

SINAN AS INTERIOR DECORATOR

Sinan's first mausoleum in Istanbul was that of Süleyman the Magnificent's Admiral Barbarossa (Hayreddin Barbaros Pasha) at Beşiktaş (948/1541–2). Subsequently, the mausolea he built were for the grandest of grandees, for Sultans, for princes (Şehzades) [Fig. 17], and for royal ladies or their commoner husbands. The entrance porch to the tomb of Süleyman the Magnificent at Süleymaniye in Istanbul, built 1567 by his son, Selim II, in the year following his death, was roofed with a series of impressively veined Proconnesian marble slabs from Hagia Sophia, now restored to its exonarthex, which had been erected to promulgate the decisions of the Byzantine Ecumenical Council of 1166 AD. (Their reuse here in such an inconspicuous position suggests opportunism rather than propaganda.) The tombs of Süleyman the Magnificent and Selim II both have double domes, the inner dome of the former covering the central arcade. This has lavish decoration outside and especially inside, of Iznik tiles, coloured glass, and a painted, relief-carved stucco dome. Outside, the mausoleum of Selim II at Ayasofya is not an octagon but a cube with chamfered corners, with four deep arched recesses or exedras inside, alternating with stalactite consoles. The passage between the two domes is emphasized outside by eight windows at the base of the outer dome. Its decoration is as rich and light as that of Süleyman and even its exterior masonry is exceptionally elegant.

Inside, these splendid Imperial mausolea made considerable use of polychrome tiles, initially *cuerda seca*, culminating in Istanbul with those of the tomb of Selim I (d. 1520) and of Şehzade Mehmed (d. 1543). Subsequently, underglaze-painted tiles made at Iznik were adopted for the tombs of Süleyman and his wife, Haseki Hürrem at Süleymaniye; Selim II, Murad III, and Mehmed III at Ayasofya; and finally Ahmed I on the Hippodrome. This fashion was almost exclusively Imperial: the tiles of Rüstem Pasha's tomb at Şehzadebaşı he must have owed, like the tiles of his mosque, to the influence of his wife, Mihrimah Sultan, the daughter of Süleyman the Magnificent and Hürrem Sultan.

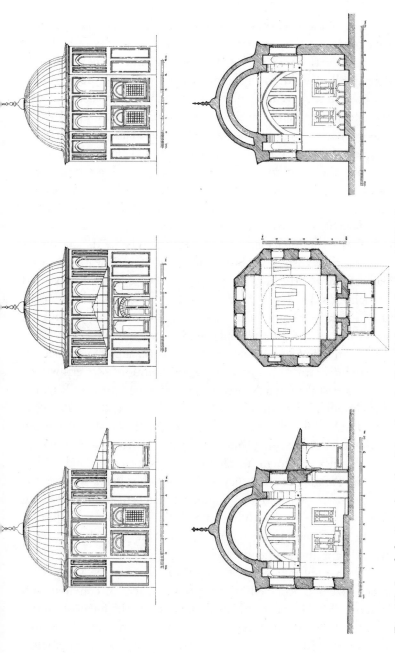

Fig. 17. Istanbul, Ayasofya, the Princes' tomb (Şehzadeler Türbesi), c.1575–80.

The glorious effects these tiles produce make it surprising that otherwise they appear only in a small minority of buildings associated with Sinan, almost all in Istanbul and Edirne and mainly concentrated inside on *mihrabs* or *qibla* walls. So great is their variety that there is little evidence for deliberate choice of pattern, though the tile panels in the mosque of Sokollu Mehmed Pasha may be a derivative of those he used in Süleymaniye. The brilliant colourism was further enhanced by painted decoration, as on the müezzins' platforms in Selimiye at Edirne and in mosques like that of Kılıç Ali Pasha at Tophane and the Valide Camii at Üsküdar, which makes lavish use of both arabesques and chinoiserie (*rûmî* and *hatâyî*) ornament to dazzling effect.

This exceptional emphasis on decoration belies the customary claims for the austerity of Sinan's interiors. If to tilework and wall-painting we add the hanging ornaments of silvered glass or painted ostrich eggs decorated in various ways, the thousands of lamps, the brilliantly coloured glass of the windows, the carpets and the woodwork of mosques like Süleymaniye, the intended effect must have been one of magnificent superabundance, almost overwhelming the architecture. What was the exact intention? Modern writers often suggest that Sinan's interiors were intended to evoke Paradise, but although historians like Celâlzâde Mustafa (*c*.896–975/1490–1567) indeed use the metaphor of Paradise they make greater use of the legendary many-columned Garden of Irem (*dhat al-'umud*) of the kings of 'Ad in Yemen, a paradise on Earth indeed but not the Paradise of the believer. On the other hand, whereas the gloom and mystery of Hagia Sophia was almost certainly intended to inspire the visitor with holy dread, the brilliance and lightness of the fenestration of Sinan's later buildings brought the outer world right inside the mosque.

In funerary architecture the tomb of Süleyman the Magnificent seems to have occupied an exceptional place. In common with practice in other parts of Hanafi Islam it was the focus of regular Qur'an readings and formal visits on anniversaries and designated days of the Muslim year; and, in common with Ottoman practice too, his wooden cenotaph was crowned with his turbans, draped with garments from his wardrobe, and adorned with weapons or jewellery too. But this was by no means all: his heroic status in the eyes of his successors, Selim II and Murad III, made it virtually the object of a cult.

That this was not wholly unenvisaged is suggested by the endowment deed of Süleymaniye (7 Receb 984/16 May 1557). There is a striking disparity between the personnel appointed to subsidiary elements of the complex, like the medical school with only eight students, and to the tombs of Süleyman and his wife, Hürrem Sultan. That of Süleyman's tomb included two keepers, one of whose duties was to supervise visitors; a gardener, to tend the tombs of Süleyman and Hürrem, and other worthies buried in the cemetery; a keeper of incense; and no fewer than a hundred and thirty four Qur'an readers and their supervisors, to ensure the continuous recitation of the Qur'an, day and night—though their salaries were small and they were evidently part-time. The unprecedented size of the staff and the cramped conditions inside the cemetery, not to speak of the tomb itself, raise an important, if now unanswerable, practical question: where did they all sit, particularly when it was raining? The considerable degree of organization required amounts practically to the creation of a ritual.

From accounts of the 1570s and 1580s for maintenance and repairs[1] we also learn of the furnishing and lighting of the tombs, especially in Ramazan and on feast days. Great candles were lavishly decorated with gold leaf and furnished with gilt metal finials and drip-trays and enormous quantities of beeswax, sesame and olive oil, and tallow allotted for them. Burnished globes, large and small, and glass lamps decorated with gold and silver foil and red ochre and with silk tassels, were hung round the tombs. Carpets were spread; and around the graves of Süleyman and Hürrem were placed blue and white pottery buckets or vases with cut flowers, roses in summer and narcissi in winter. In addition to these luxurious furnishings substantial quantities of incense were burned, and on feast days those involved in the recital of the

[1] Cf. Rogers, 1999.

Qur'an and other texts were well provided with sugar, buns (çörek, simid), musk, cinnamon, cloves, fresh and dried fruit, rose-water, and lemonade. Nothing was spared. The provision for lighting, gratuities, and treats in accounts for the ceremonies in the mosque of Süleymaniye and at the tombs on one single evening in Ramazan amounted to 3332 akçe; the total monthly outgoings of the hospital of the complex were a mere 9000 akçe.

The gardener's responsibilities did not end with the tending of the graves in the cemetery. He also supervised a staff of Acemioğlans tilling its garden, which, like the gardens of the mosque, were planted with fruit trees. This was in part an economic matter, for flowers and fruit from the gardens of Süleymaniye were to be sold for the benefit of the foundation. It was evidently here too that the cut flowers for the tombs were grown.

BRIDGES, BATHS, AND CARAVANSARAYS

Both bridges and baths (hamams) are relevant to Sinan's waterworks. Baths, in certain quarters of Istanbul at least, were open to a public without distinction of religion, for example, in Jewish quarters they were largely used by Jews. Some, moreover, like that of Mihal Beg at Edirne described by Evliyâ Çelebi, where leather was dyed sky blue, red, yellow, pink, and orange, were provided with separate industrial sections—rather surprisingly, considering the stink they must have made. In nineteenth-century restorations hamams in particular often underwent radical modifications of plan, making it difficult to say how far Sinan's baths were original. Plans tend to be standard, however, and divergences from them not easy to explain. Among Sinan's more famous baths is the double bath, one half for men and the other for women, he built for Hürrem Sultan at Ayasofya (964/1556-7), near the site of the Baths of Zeuxippus built by Septimius Severus (c.196 AD) and enlarged by Constantine, possibly making use of its water supply. The entrance halls or apodyteria are at either end with impressive domes: these narrow domed corridors lead to separate hot rooms with private rooms leading off from them. It was commercially extremely successful, bringing in more than 80,000 akçe in revenue each year.

Bridges were among Sinan's earliest commissions. Although Kuran questions Sinan's part in the bridge built for Lutfî Pasha over the River Pruth in thirteen days on the Moldavian campaign in 1538, he unreservedly accepts that in 935/1528–9 he built the bridge at Uzunköprü (Svilengrad in Bulgaria) for the Grand Vizier, Çoban Mustafa Pasha. Bridges remained important among his responsibilities throughout his career. In 1563 Süleyman, returning from hunting in the marshes west of Istanbul, was nearly drowned in a flood while crossing the lagoons at Çekmece. This led in 1566 to a series of urgent orders to build a bridge (actually four bridges connected by a paved causeway) across it [Fig. 18], for the Sultan's projected Hungarian campaign, where he was to meet his death. This was completed in late Safer 975/early September 1567, using materials from the stores at Süleymaniye at a cost of almost 11 million akçe, with a caravansaray, shops, and a bakery added the following year. Sinan is also reported by Sâ'î to have built the famous Vişegrad bridge over the Drina in Bosnia for Sokollu Mehmed Pasha (dated 985/1577–8). These bridges were not merely an essential element of the Ottoman campaign roads. At the head of each, and at Uzunköprü too, there was originally a major caravansaray, though only that at Büyük Çekmece now survives.

Of the thirty-one caravansarays attributed to Sinan in all three treatises on his works, thirteen bear the names of Grand Viziers, and of these Sokollu Mehmed Pasha is especially noteworthy for those he built between urban centres on campaign routes to the Balkans. Because of the difficulty of moving men and materials in the rain and snow of winter their use tended to be seasonal, but they doubtless attracted merchants and foreign ambassadors travelling to or from Edirne and Istanbul at other times of the year. None of his caravansarays survives in its entirety, but the most interesting of them is the port and complex built in 982/ 1574–5 at Payas (the modern Yakacık) in Cilicia on the Adana– Aleppo road, which, though later much rebuilt, gives a fair idea

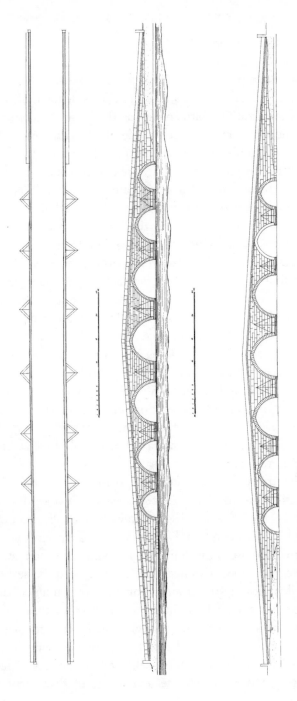

Fig. 18. Büyük Çekmece. Bridge (975/1567–8).

of its original layout [Fig. 19]. It lay on probably the most important Ottoman trade route of the later sixteenth century, bringing raw silk from the Caspian to Aleppo and thence to the looms at Bursa and in Istanbul, and to the Northern Mediterranean. The Venetians, and later the French and the English Levant Company, all had permanent consulates at Aleppo, with resident merchant colonies trading fine woollens for the silk and exporting it westwards by sea to Europe.

The problem was that Aleppo was at least three or four days' distance from the Mediterranean. The Venetians had long used the port of Tripoli (Trablus in the Lebanon) where already in the late fifteenth century they had established a consulate: Sokollu Mehmed's initiative suggests that he was attempting to divert the foreign trade, from which port dues would have been immensely profitable. Being in a sparsely populated area the foundation at Payas had to be self-sufficient: it was, therefore, not just a caravansaray and a closed market (*arasta*) but, like a great urban foundation, was centred on a mosque, with a *medrese*, a double bath, and an *imaret* as well [Fig. 19]. The international sea trade was governed, as Fernand Braudel showed in his study of the Mediterranean in the time of Philip II of Spain, by the sailing season, which ran from April to October; however, the overland trade to northwest Anatolia was all the year round and would have been periodically swollen by pilgrims on their way to Damascus and thence to Makka. Consequently the staff of the foundation, the Customs officials, the accountants, and the garrison must have been permanent, and their needs were reflected in the scale and amenities of the foundation. Interestingly, although the Payas project amounted to a major exercise in rural regeneration and its constitution was accordingly ambitious, its architecture is modest and it is built in the style of many unassuming buildings of the Adana–Antioch area (the modern province of Hatay). That in itself is not enough to disprove Sinan's involvement, for, as Kuban has observed, his projects, like the Takiyya al-Sulaymaniyya at Damascus, the execution of which was delegated to junior members of his office, tended to be

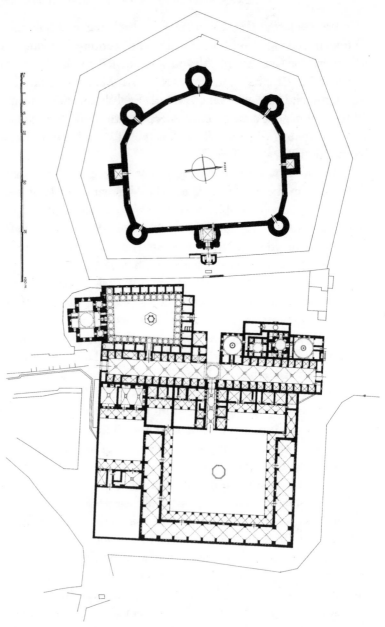

Fig. 19. Payas (Yakacık), on the Mediterranean east of Adana. Mosque, imaret, and caravansaray for Sokollu Mehmed Pasha (982/1574–5).

relatively uncomplicated and suited to the work of local builders and masons.

Unfortunately, we have little evidence so far of how well the foundation at Payas worked, and it passes without mention in the accounts of contemporary European travellers like the botanist and physician Leonard Rauwolff. The coastal plains of Cilician were malarial at this time and, quite probably, it was abandoned by Sokollu Mehmed's successors after his assassination in 1579. By the seventeenth century the port had silted up and the emporium had moved to the nearby harbour of Alexandretta (Iskenderun), which was equally malarial but which outside the sailing season was uninhabited.

5

Sinan as planner
palaces and religious foundations

Istanbul from the foundation of Byzantium in the sixth century BC had rejoiced in its geographical situation. It commanded the Bosphorus, which separated Europe and Asia, and a narrow inlet, the Golden Horn, well protected by a rocky promontory, which offered a safe harbour against the appalling storms of the long winter. Mehmed II exploited its topography when (c.1465) he began his new palace (now known as the Topkapı Saray) overlooking simultaneously the Sea of Marmara, the Golden Horn, and the Bosphorus, with the church of Hagia Sophia only just outside its walls. The city afforded more, however. Built, like Rome, on seven hills it was a standing invitation to an architect with an eye for a prospect, and Mehmed II's repopulation of the Byzantine city was to be complemented in the sixteenth century by Sinan's splendidly numerous urban buildings. With the exception of palaces these were practically all Islamic and religious in character. The substantial populations of Greeks, Armenians, and Jews had no access to him and, for reasons of security, were encouraged progressively to settle in their own quarters up the Golden Horn or in proximity with the Italians in Galata, the former Genoese suburb of Pera.

Modern architects as planners see themselves as creators of an urban environment, preferably on virgin soil if their grandest schemes are to be fully realized. Such concerns were very far from Sinan. Ottoman Istanbul was certainly not *un*planned, but its development was a complex process. The radical measures taken by Mehmed the Conqueror to repopulate the city imposed many immediate changes. Subsequently Ottoman Court architects were made well aware of the effects of the major Imperial projects on their surroundings, though, with the exception of certain public areas like the Hippodrome and streets like the Divan Yolu, they can have had little opportunity to conceive or execute buildings that took their immediate surroundings into account. The Istanbul that faced Sinan on his appointment in 1537 was not so much a homogeneous city as a congeries of individual complexes planned in detail but linked by labyrinths of streets. At his death, thanks to his office, there were far more of them and they were even grander. But it would be an anachronism to describe Sinan as an urbanist in the modern sense.

Sinan's contribution to *Ottoman* urbanism was, paradoxically perhaps, most conspicuous in the palaces he built. His works in the Topkapı Saray, which are particularly associated with repairs to the Imperial kitchens following a major fire in 1574 and, perhaps simultaneously, with major extensions to the Harem quarters, have evoked most attention and, in Murad III's view anyway, must have been the most important. Moreover, although the palace of Ibrahim Pasha on the Hippodrome (built 1521–4) is the only sixteenth-century minister's palace to survive in Istanbul, Sinan's numerous works on palaces—especially for the royal ladies and for the ministers of Süleyman the Magnificent, Selim II and Murad III—are listed with only minor discrepancies by all the biographical treatises. They included schools for the Imperial pages like the Galata Saray; pleasure pavilions or grandstands, like Süleyman's palaces at Üsküdar and the Silivri Gate (neither of which survives), to review the army at the outset of a campaign; and hunting lodges inside and outside Istanbul. Palaces are not so much respecters as creators of the urban environment. The site selected, the constituent elements and their ultimate appearance were not only subject to patron and architect, but because they were also great administrative centres with hordes of servants, slaves, staff, and conscripted tradesmen, as well as stables, outbuildings, and extensive gardens or farms, their effects on their surroundings were far-reaching. Even on more open sites, Müller-Wiener has remarked, the royal palaces of Sinan's time, like the long-vanished Üsküdar palace, the Kavak Saray, with which Sinan was certainly involved, not only exploited sea views commanding both the Bosphorus and the Marmara; their landscaping may well have been even more important than the pavilions or dwellings within their walls. Indeed, Mustafa Âlî, writing in the 1580s, bases one of his arguments for the decline of the Ottoman empire in his time on the extravagance of successive Sultans in the building and maintenance of their palaces.

Most of our information on these comes from contemporary travellers and historians and Ottoman registers of repairs and maintenance, but it suggests that Istanbul as a city of palaces was no less grand than Cairo under the Mamluk Sultans or Rome under the Renaissance Popes. We know that they were particularly concentrated on the Divan Yolu, the processional route from Ayasofya to Süleymaniye, and on the Hippodrome, where on the south side they were cleared away when the complex of Ahmed I was built. Palace architecture is, however, inherently ephemeral and the borderline between pavilion and folly has never been carefully drawn. At best they were subject to radical alteration or even total destruction at an owner's whim; and being half-timbered or largely of wood, were highly vulnerable to the periodic fires that ravaged Istanbul. The palaces Sinan built for the four Viziers of the Dome were evidently official residences that passed to a vizier's successor on his retirement, dismissal, or death, and their maintenance accordingly figures in seventeenth-century account books too. However, many palaces, particularly those where a vizier was not protected by marriage alliances to the Imperial family, were, on one pretext or another, confiscated by the State, turned to other purposes, or, sometimes, razed to the ground to provide space for a pious foundation. Sokollu Mehmed Pasha (assassinated 1579), for example, had a palace at Ayasofya that was sold by his heirs to Ahmed I in 1018/1609, the year works began on the Blue Mosque, for demolition to allow work to continue. The Kadırga palace, built either for him or for his wife, Esmahan Sultan, a daughter of Selim II (d. 1585) seems on the other hand to have been a private residence, for it remained in the hands of their heirs till it was acquired by Ahmed III in 1724.

In chronicling the construction of Şehzade [Fig. 20],[1] Celâlzâde Mustafa refers to what seems like a competition, where brilliant engineers and architects presented architectural drawings and plans to the Sultan, who selected those that pleased him most, i.e. Sinan's. There is, however, no other evidence for this practice at the Ottoman court and Sinan, once in place as Court Architect, would scarcely have permitted his authority to be challenged in this way. To suggest that the choice was the Sultan's could therefore be sheer flattery, for the choice of a particular plan can scarcely have been of much consequence to him. But even if Sinan had no competition here he may have submitted alternative designs, and justified the one that the Sultan finally chose. With foundations on such a vast scale both constituent buildings and their internal planning were often major preoccupations. He doubtless also played an important role in deciding what their constituent foundations were to be. These varied from the deeply pious to the highly practical, and a basic decision, by Sinan or his patron, was to determine the elements required and what importance to give each. As far as the constituent elements went, some were standard or dictated by State policy. The Ottoman *ilmiye* system, as instituted by Mehmed II, required candidates for the highest legal office to proceed through a series of *medreses*, and the four *medreses* attached to Süleymaniye were an extension of this *cursus honorum*. Elements could also have been ad hoc—a hospital for a favourite physician, or a *medrese* or a School of Tradition (*Dârü'l-Hadîs*) for an esteemed scholar. Sinan's vast practical experience, in any case, fitted him

[1]Kappert 1981, p. 44. [fo. 377^b] Mühendisân-i kâmil ve mü'essisân-i Aristo şemâ'il muctema' olub etvâr-i ğarîbede resimler ve tarhlar bünyad edüb getürdiler.

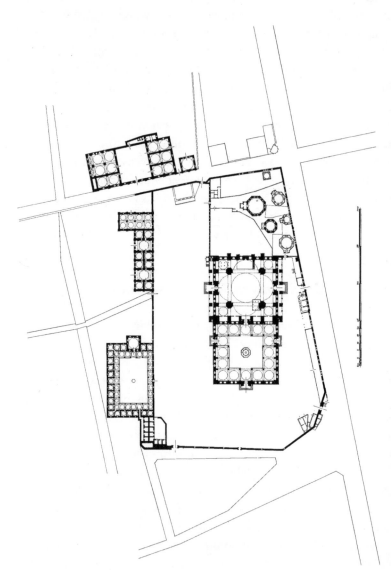

Fig. 20. Istanbul, Şehzadebaşı. Complex (külliye) of Şehzade (inaugurated 955/1548–9. Mosque, medrese, mekteb, imaret, cemetery and caravansaray.

exceptionally well for an advisory role and the choice of components for his Istanbul foundations, as well as their actual buildings, may often largely have been his.

When we think of Sinan as a planner rather than an urbanist, however, we immediately turn to Süleymaniye, Süleyman the Magnificent's great foundation in Istanbul (inaugurated 1557). Like the palaces, the buildings of Süleymaniye dominate both the Golden Horn and the Sea of Marmara. At the centre of a great esplanade is the mosque in a walled garden, fronted by a courtyard and backed by a walled cemetery with the mausolea [Fig. 21] of Hürrem Sultan (d. 1558) and of Süleyman himself (d. 1566, completed 1567). Round the esplanade are disposed four *medreses*; a *hamam*; a School of Tradition (*Dârü'l-Hadîs*) and a School of Qur'an-reading (*Dârü'l-Kurrâ'*); a Qur'an-school; a medical school; a hospital; a caravansaray and a soup kitchen (*imaret*), some of them spilling over, as it were, and built down the slopes towards the Golden Horn—perhaps deliberately to reinforce the impression of spaciousness.

The Süleymaniye account books, though they cover only the later years of building-works and omit, therefore, the landscaping and digging of foundations, which would have provided additional information on points where Sinan's personal direction was of crucial importance for the result, are a virtually inexhaustible source for both architectural practice and the administration of the building trades in the mid-sixteenth century. They clearly demonstrate Sinan's priorities and the financial constraints upon them.

The principal register covers the period 1 Muharrem 961–Şa'bân 966/7 December 1553–9 March 1559, and evidently represents the final settlement when the books were closed and the accounts were presented to the Sultan. The total expenditure of 26,251,939 akçe covers wholesale purchases of building materials, wages and salaries for the conscripted labour force, the administrators and the clerical staff, transport and extraordinary expenses, and probable afterthoughts, such as a large purchase of lead on the open market. In the face of such a colossal enterprise miscalculations must have been rife, and it is scarcely a criticism

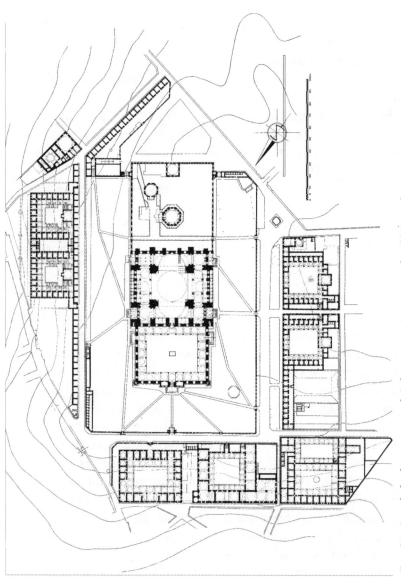

Fig. 21. Istanbul, the mosque of *Süleymaniye (inaugurated 1557) and its appurtenances.*

of Sinan that some of his estimates may have been defective or too low.

The highly centralized character of the Ottoman bureaucracy at this time did not exclude a considerable measure of improvization, not to speak of impromptu cover-ups. Ottoman accounting in the sixteenth century, moreover, evolved continuously, and we should not ignore the possibility that another of Sinan's prime contributions to Ottoman architectural practice was the keeping of exact accounts. Fortunately, they formed the model for the building accounts of the mosque of Ahmed I (the Blue Mosque) in Istanbul, for to accompany these a collection of Imperial edicts and other documents (Topkapı Saray Library H. 1424) relating to works on Süleymaniye was compiled by Kalender Pasha, Ahmed I's Clerk of the Works. Without this manual the accounts for Süleymaniye, to him no less than to us, would have been extremely difficult to follow.

Like the sixteenth-century Oxford college foundations established by successive Chancellors of England for the training of officials for the highest offices of state, the *medreses* and other foundations associated with Süleymaniye were private institutions. Where pious foundations built by Sinan included caravansarays, as at Lüleburgaz in Turkish Thrace and at the Atik Valide complex at Üsküdar, these were undeniably public, though we do not know whether they were free or paying and they may have played other roles too. As at Lüleburgaz they also served as barracks when the army was on campaign or the Court was on the move to Edirne or Filibe (Plovdiv in Bulgaria). Or, like the latter, they might be strategically placed at ports or landings on the international trade routes, and would, like the *fondachi* in contemporary Venice, also have been where the immensely profitable taxes on trade with Europe and the East were levied.

It is, however, not always entirely clear which elements were public. Take the soup kitchen (*imaret*), which was a conspicuous feature of the Süleymaniye complex. It is difficult to identify kitchen areas in the subsidiary appurtenances of the complex, and given the size of the whole foundation and the lavish provisions allotted to it, the *imaret* could well have catered only for the staff employed there. Had it been primarily intended for the public, moreover, it would have brought in a large number of disreputable outsiders several times daily, which could well have encouraged disorderly behaviour—and, to judge from the present name of one of the streets on the Süleymaniye plaza, Tiryaki Çarşısı (the Market of the Opium-Addicts) that is what later occurred. And even if *imarets* in Ottoman Turkey were mostly public it does not follow that those attached to the great Imperial foundations were public too.

In the case of Süleymaniye the seven-year building period certainly allowed for significant afterthoughts. The building site was, for example, enlarged by further acquisitions of land as late as 1552, when the mosque and several other buildings of the complex were already under construction, doubtless at the edge of the vast artificial terrace and hence to give more space for the *medreses* running down towards the Golden Horn. In that same year we read of the addition of a hospital to the complex, and a new site for the School of Tradition, the original positioning of which was too cramped for the number of students envisaged (though the new site, to judge from the extant building, does not seem to have been much better). When the surviving account books begin, moreover, in 1553, although the soup kitchen (*imaret*) and the hospital are stated to be under construction nothing is said of the *medreses*. One of these at least was certainly an afterthought, for in the endowment deed only three, not four, are described.

How far was the diversion of Ottoman State funds into architecture a more rational, economical, or equitable policy than alternative forms of expenditure, private or public? The question is, of course, anachronistic, for Sinan was merely the agent of Imperial beneficence that was one of the traditional attributes of the just Muslim ruler. There has been a persistent current of Muslim thought that disapproves of grand building projects, but beneficence must have its grand side too, and it makes little sense to enquire whether cheaper projects would have fitted Sinan's, or his patrons', purpose better. With current building styles and technology the materials left little room for economy. The penalties for the collapse of a dome or other public failure in Imperial Ottoman architecture were so alarming that Ottoman architects had no alternative but to build with exaggerated safety factors: indeed, the rarity of structural defects in Sinan's extant works, despite their often problematic siting and inevitable earthquake damage, is a clear demonstration of his caution.

Grand as it was, Süleymaniye was no folly [Fig. 22]. The total of 26 million akçe (or something like 580,000 Venetian gold ducats) for the accounts for the years 961–6/1553–9, which Barkan estimates as about 49 per cent of the whole costs, was—at estimates for 1530—little more than one-sixteenth of the Ottoman empire's annual income and rather less than the annual income from Egypt alone. Of the total, moreover, 26 million akçe was from the Sultan's *private* purse, and if we consider that a Venetian gold crown sold to him in 1532 by a consortium of Venetian merchants may have cost him as much as 115,000 ducats, Süleymaniye—even including the costs of the Kâğıthane and later the Kırkçeşme waterworks and the repairs and maintenance of the three hundred fountains the latter provided for—scarcely seems extravagant. Moreover, even if it was indeed essentially a private foundation, its side effects were markedly to the public benefit.

More relevant to the question of 'cost-effectiveness' is the diversion of men and materials to the construction of Imperial complexes. By good luck, perhaps, rather than good management, the building of Süleymaniye did not coincide with major campaigns on any of the Ottoman fronts. This was probably just as well. For the procedures attending the acquisition of four monolithic granite columns for Süleymaniye in 1551 were at the very least extravagant [Fig. 23]. These involved the construction of a special quay at Alexandria with timber sent from the forests behind the Dardanelles; the building of two heavy naval transport ships (one of them apparently lost on the return journey from Alexandria) in the Dardanelles dockyards; and, the following year, further reinforcement of quays at Tripoli (Trablus in the Lebanon) and

Fig. 22. Melchior Lorichs (Lorck), portrait of Süleyman the Magnificent, with the mosque of Süleymaniye in the background (c.1558). London, British Museum, Department of Prints and Drawings 1848 11–25 24. Courtesy of the Trustees of the British Museum.

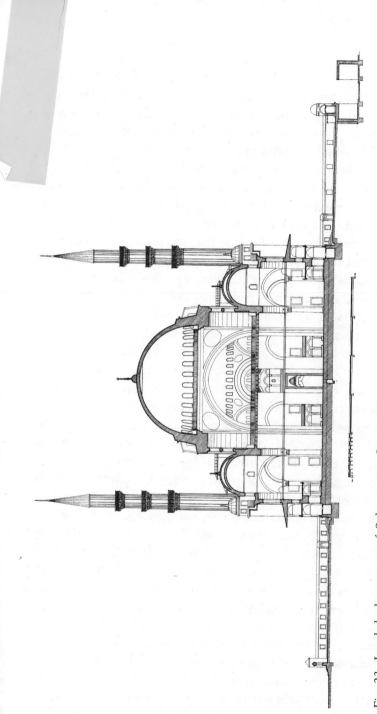

Fig. 23. Istanbul, the mosque of Süleymaniye. Cross-section.

yet more ships for columns brought over the Lebanon on sledges from the temple of Jupiter at Baalbek to make up the number required. The costs were envisaged as falling upon provincial revenues, which perhaps in normal periods of civil quiescence could easily have been absorbed. However, had the authorities known beforehand of the time, trouble, and expense of obtaining the columns they could scarcely have issued orders to bring them from Alexandria in the first place, all the more so in that they involved the diversion of artillery ships and labour in the already overstretched dockyards of the Dardanelles. It is difficult, indeed, to avoid the impression that the exercise was a bungle: however, the edicts it provoked are surprisingly uncritical in tone and Gülru Necipoğlu-Kafadar may perhaps be right to parallel this frenzied activity with Justinian's collecting of marbles for Hagia Sophia from far and wide in the Classical world.

Admittedly the organization of Ottoman building trade worked in Sinan's favour. The specification of much of the timber and building stone for Sinan's complexes by function and cut indicates a considerable degree of standardization at the quarries and the timberyards. This undoubtedly saved much labour, and the practice must have extended considerably during Sinan's tenure of office, with the constant need to build bigger and faster. The provision of strategic materials like iron for girders (mainly from Samokov in Bulgaria) and lead for cramps or covering roofs (from Siderokastron in Northern Greece and elsewhere) was, however, problematic, because the centralized organization of mining and its traditional technology made the supply highly unresponsive to fluctuations in demand. Lead was particularly urgent since if it were not immediately available for cramps it could have delayed completion of a building by months, even years, and because Süleyman's major foundations had to compete simultaneously with works on the Topkapı Saray and other royal palaces. The problem was solved partly by recourse to the open market, which evidently flourished in partnership with State-leased concessions, and partly by juggling with lead and iron acquired for other projects, borrowing from some to cope with immediate requirements and paying them back when the pressure had eased. Recourse to the market was not as paradoxical as might appear for, as Sir William Harborne reported in 1579, there were periodic gluts of imported lead, though the insatiable military demand for munitions makes it unlikely that much of that found its way into the building trade. That work continued so rapidly and smoothly, in spite of the many conflicting demands for strategic materials, demonstrates yet another facet of Sinan's genius as planner and master of the Sultans' works.

6

Sinan's style and his use of architectural decoration

Though, as I have argued above, Sinan's taste for interior decoration was far from austere, what most strikes the observer of Sinan's mosques from the outside is the sobriety of their contrasts—between the pyramidal piles of geometrical forms with subtle contrasts of grey (travertine and lead) and the stalactite decoration of minarets and portal canopies; between horizontal and vertical space; and between vertical walls and curvilinear domes and semi-domes. Even as compared with Hagia Sophia Sinan's great mosques studiously avoid contrasts of bold colour. This exterior perspicuousness seems to balance the abundance of light inside.

It might seem easy enough to tell that a building was executed by Sinan, or at least no more difficult than to attribute a building on stylistic grounds to Palladio, Borromini, or Wren. But the grounds usually advanced—the adaptation of an overall plan to exploit or compensate for features of irregular topography; the combination of structural forms to give novelty of structure, as well as variety of appearance; the articulation of exterior side façades; the use of windows to give maximum brilliance inside; and the adroit choice of materials (though here the ultimate choice may not have been his)—may be too unspecific to distinguish Sinan's works from those of his predecessors or successors. Stylistic evidence, such as door, window, and cornice mouldings; the profiling of door recesses and side niches; the composition and detailing of stalactite hoods, pendants, balcony consoles, finials, and pediments; has so far not been exploited. This is partly to be explained by the Western European architectural movements of the past two generations, which have tended to decry, or at least ignore, the use of decoration on or in buildings. They cannot, however, be ignored.

In projects like Süleymaniye, where the costings for precious marbles, granite columns, fine woods, and Iznik tiles demonstrate Sinan's concern for the visual effects of colour and surface, he obviously did not leave architectural ornament to take care of itself. The highly decorated façade of the tomb of Şehzade Mehmed at Şehzadebaşı indicates that already by the 1540s he was experimenting with a decorative canon [Fig. 24]. This could never have been achieved without close centralized control, for increasing standardization demanded by economy of labour, time, and materials also increased the danger that glaring disparities in style or technique would lead to visual incoherence. The Court Architect's office was also very vulnerable to the demands of campaign duty. A case in point was the four hundred master builders and carpenters called for service on Murad III's Persian campaign,[1] which created a shortage of qualified craftsmen to maintain and repair the walls of Istanbul and the Imperial pious foundations and demanded the recruiting of six hundred craftsmen from the island of Mytilene. The edict, for once, does not seem to be very practical, because mass recruitment of this sort works best with unskilled labour: it would have been more prudent to send these recruits off on campaign (where they would mostly have been employed on fortifications), leaving the experienced craftsmen in Istanbul. Such practices further increased the danger of visual incoherence.

The Süleymaniye accounts break down the building works by reference to the various parts of the complex on which work was proceeding, and to operations paid specially at piece work rates. The latter included door and window cornices, stalactites

---

[1] BBA *MD* 49, p. 50 no.171, Rebî'ülâhir 991/1Apr.–May 1583.

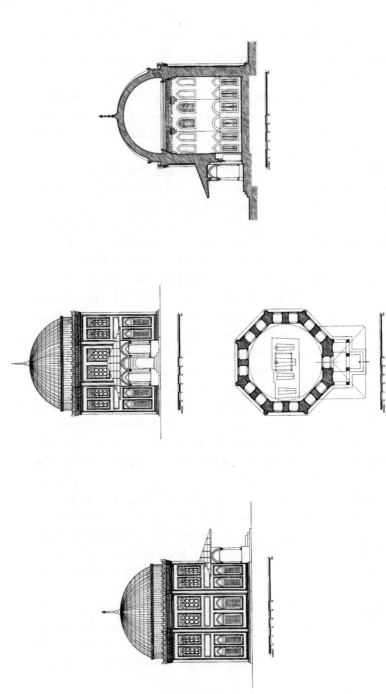

Fig. 24. Istanbul, Şehzadebaşı, the mausoleum of Şehzade Mehmed (950/1543–4).

(*mukarnas*) and pendants, and the minarets. These last can easily be shown to have been specialist work, not only because of peculiarities in their decoration like the high-relief knot motifs on the minarets of Şehzade, which do not recur in other parts of the building, or on any other of Sinan's minarets, but also because of the exceptional knowledge of statics that their stability demanded and the need to coordinate their decoration, notably of their stalactite balconies, with the structure. However, to judge from the accounts, no one group of craftsmen seems to have been responsible for stalactites, and different gangs, sometimes of only one or two craftsmen, were paid for stalactite capitals, consoles for balconies, belvederes, or projecting upper windows and stalactite porches.

Other works on which pieceworkers were employed included the cornice of the fountain in the courtyard, the frames of round windows for the mosque, and the cornices of the upper windows, banisters, and grilles. Their pay does not seem to have been in proportion to the superior skill required, though those who carved the openwork pendant globes for the stalactite porches of the mosque and other constituents of the Süleymaniye complex were clearly virtuosi and treated as such: their daily wages were considerably higher not only than those of the other masons but also than the permanent staff of the Court Architect's office.

The diversity of specialization, the smallness of the gangs, and the urgency of works inevitably raise the question, how were they organized? Scarcely like the cathedral builders of medieval Europe who, in the face of setbacks or natural disasters, abandoned their work to take it up again in a different style, happily juxtaposing details, and even structures, of different dates. We have seen that in the Ottoman building trade building materials such as wood, stone, and (less unexpectedly) brick are described for the most part in standardized terms. Stone certainly arrived blocked out from the quarries, which were mostly worked by prisoners or convicts, so that much of the work in the builder's yard at Süleymaniye must have been a finishing process; but what happened with window frames, for example? How did the forced labourers in the quarries know what to do? At this point we have no evidence on the Ottoman side and have to turn to contemporary practice in Italy, where, providentially, the building accounts for the Strozzi palace in Florence (begun 1489) survive. These have been ably analysed by Richard Goldthwaite.

Here in communication between architects and masons models played an essential role. We naturally think of the scale models of buildings that are among the glories of Renaissance woodwork. These, however, generally had neither a practical nor a structural purpose, being much like the 'presentation drawings' executed in modern architects' offices for their clients when a project has been agreed. The practical models were of details, like those Filarete describes in his *Treatise on Architecture* 'of the building's ornaments that I wanted done first, basements, cornices, architraves and doors'. They need not have been complicated: templates or sometimes mere profiles would usually have sufficed. These were portable, could be made in as many copies as necessary and, even if the work was contracted out, could be sent to both the quarries and to the builders' yards, harmonizing and coordinating their work from the very start. Though it is not possible to demonstrate this procedure for more than a handful of Renaissance buildings, the organization of works on Palazzo Strozzi must have been standard Northern Italian practice. Moreover, since the execution of mouldings, cornices, architraves, and capitals was under identical constraints in contemporary Ottoman Istanbul it is difficult to see how Sinan could have organized the work in any other way.

Whether or not Sinan made such models himself, who made them if he did not, or who can be regarded as the actual designers of the architectural ornament, is scarcely worth consideration at the present moment when the work of recording and analysing architectural details has hardly begun. In any case, the buildings of Bayazid II at Edirne and in Istanbul, the work of his Court Architect Ya'kubşah, and Selimiye in Istanbul, attributed to the first Court Architect of Süleyman's reign, Ali the Persian (Acem Ali), demonstrate that there was a lively repertoire, possibly even a canon, of all sorts of appropriate details from which Sinan, or the craftsmen delegated by him, could draw on for inspiration.

Templates and models would have been subject to hard use and have not survived. Although decorative details certainly recur in Sinan's buildings it is rather difficult to determine which designs he regarded as standard. We may, however, note a tendency for interior surface decoration to reappear on exteriors, like the splendid inscription roundels in Iznik tiles on the *qibla* walls of both Süleymaniye and the mosque of Sokollu Mehmed Pasha [Fig. 25], which are then reinterpreted in shallow relief on the courtyard façade of Selimiye. Again, there is a striking similarity between the decoration of the pediments of the entrances of Süleymaniye, both into the courtyard and into the mosque, and the back of a campaign throne made for Süleyman veneered with ebony, ivory, and mother of pearl [Figs. 25 and 26]. It could well be objected that such recurrences are too few or too disparate to suggest a special connection with Sinan; but there is much more work to be done before we even speak of a corpus of sixteenth-century architectural ornament, let alone motifs and devices particular to Sinan.

Among the earlier commissions of Sinan's career the order to execute a marble *minbar* for the Great Mosque at Esztergom following Süleyman's victorious Hungarian campaign of 1542–3 may be particularly revealing. It was especially important since it involved the conversion of the Cathedral, with the tombs of the Hungarian kings, into a mosque, a transformation rich with symbolism of Ottoman power. Though carpentry is known to have been an important element of Sinan's early training there is no evidence that he had time to specialize as a marble carver (*mermerî, mermerci*) and it is most probable that the execution was passed on to one of the Court Architects, such as Mustafa b. Nebi in the Süleymaniye[2] works, whose speciality that was. This specialization must have referred to the *minbar*, otherwise

[2]BBA *MD* 2, p.101 nos.1036–7, 20 Şa'bân 963/30 Jun. 1556.

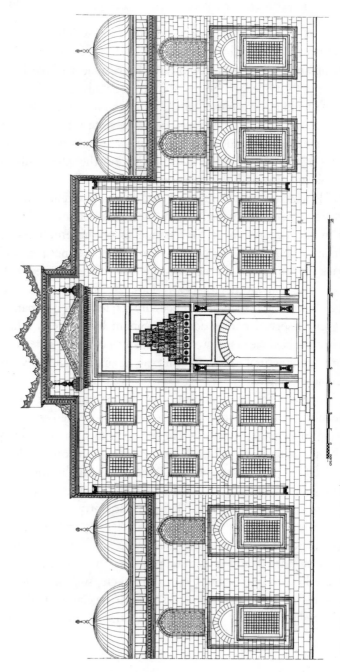

Fig. 25. Istanbul, mosque of Süleymaniye. Main gateway into the courtyard. Elevation.

Fig. 26. *Campaign throne of Süleyman the Magnificent (c.1560). Walnut inlaid with ebony, ivory and mother of pearl. Istanbul Topkapı Saray Museum 2/2879.*

the task could have been left to the masons working on the fabric. But the design of the *minbar* was as important as its execution. Whereas pre-Ottoman and early Ottoman *minbars* were of wood, and often signed by craftsmen, the *minbars* of Sinan's time, though never signed, were not just furniture—like the müezzins' rostrum inside mosques like Süleymaniye or pulpits for readers or preachers during Ramazan—but great monumental compositions, whose proportions and scale, in his largest buildings at least, seem to have been directly related to the buildings in which they were installed. That is, they were a matter of architectural, not just decorative, concern and the curious fact that in the Süleymaniye accounts the *minbar* is not costed as such may well be an indication that it was Sinan's direct responsibility. Their exploitation of solid geometry and their primarily *architectural* decoration thus makes them central to any discussion of Sinan's personal style.

Though we only have evidence for plans or elevations of one of Sinan's buildings, namely for (the mosque of) Süleymaniye, they almost certainly typify his method. The terms given by Celâlzâde Mustafa in his *Tabakâtü'l-Memâlik*[3] are ambiguous, but we have independent evidence for an elevation from the *Sûrnâme* of the poet Intizâmî depicting the celebrations of the circumcision of Murad III's sons in 1582 (Topkapı Saray Library H. 1344), where the builders or architects are shown carrying it in procession before the Sultan, as well as in an illustrated history of Süleyman's reign, the *Süleymânnâme*, also made for Murad III [Figs. 6–7]. This must be the *kârnâme* in the Süleymaniye building accounts for which substantial amounts of paper, ink, and gold leaf are allotted, for a mere plan or programme of works could not possibly have cost so much. Whether it was an elevation or a three-dimensional model is difficult to say. However, paper or cardboard castles for mock sieges, actually large enough for a token garrison of defenders, were built for other festivities in the Hippodrome and are illustrated in Matrakçı Nasuh's *Tuhfetü'l-Guzât* written in 936/1529–30 (Süleymaniye Library, Istanbul, Esat Efendi 2206 fos. 33b–34a), so

[3]Fo. 519a.

the construction of even quite a large three-dimensional model (not, of course, necessarily to scale) would have been perfectly feasible. In grand Imperial projects the architect had to have something to still the Sultan's impatience and in the circumstances the grander the model was the better.

These considerations suggest that it is not only useless but actually misleading to concentrate on the style of Sinan's buildings as a whole. In this Sinan presents an interesting parallel to Vanbrugh (1664–1726), a gifted amateur turned bewilderingly eclectic professional. While still in his early twenties, Vanbrugh is known to have spent a period of time in the East India Company's factory at Surat, and various of his sketches show a familiarity with and interest in Indian architecture. In 1699, untried and untaught, he embarked on Castle Howard, collaborating with William Talman and Nicholas Hawksmoor. This dazzling rise to eminence was crowned in 1702 by his appointment as successor to Talman as Comptroller of the Queen's Works.

Hawksmoor's draughtsmanship, detailing, and management were essential for the realization of Vanbrugh's project. This could not, however, entirely conceal his architectural inexperience. The effect of Blenheim (completed after June 1716, when he had resigned from the project), for example, depended less on the regular articulation of the Classical orders than on variety of shape and contrasting projections and recessions in both plan and silhouette, and on sudden dramatic accents furnished by towers, attics, and finials, making it more a piece of sculpture than a building. With Vanbrugh—as with Palladio and Wren, therefore, and with Sinan too—style can do little to define the way in which the architect expresses himself. The automatic tendency among historians of art and architecture to assume that we can attribute a work purely on the basis of its style is here scarcely more than a prejudice.

7

Standardization, modularity, and proportion

In this study I have had occasion to stress Sinan's practicality. Whatever statements his buildings made to his contemporaries it was the building, not the statement, that took priority. Sometimes, as I have argued in the case of Süleymaniye, we can plausibly guess their intended effect and, sometimes, though very rarely, we have his words as reported by Mustafa Sâ'î, as with Hagia Sophia, the dome of which he claimed was surpassed by Selimiye at Edirne in both height and diameter. This at least suggests his aim, but, oddly, the claim is false on both counts. Whether the error was his or Sâ'î's it is difficult to explain, since the astronomer Takiyüddin, the head of Murad III's short-lived observatory in Istanbul in the 1570s, succeeded despite the complexity of the operation resulting from its irregular configuration in accurately measuring the height and diameter of the dome of Hagia Sophia.

This anecdote brings up an additional complication, namely the extreme diversity of weights and measures over the Ottoman empire, which varied not only from city to city but from craft to craft and commodity to commodity. This was particularly the case with the cubit (*arşın*, Arabic *dhira'*), with decimal fractions. This was the standard unit of length used in surveying in Istanbul, but not only was there a specific builders' cubit (*bennâ arşını*); it elongated steadily, Alpay Özdural has ingeniously calculated, from 72.1 cm circa 1520 to 73.4 cm circa 1575. This latter was the value of Takiyüddin's cubit, which may have been kept as a standard ruler in his observatory. In the seventeenth century Court Architects came to be presented with their official cubit rule as a badge of their appointment. We do not know whether Sinan had his own, but, given the potential chaos resulting from divergence in measurements, he must have had access to the standard rule, and have been given authority to impose the measure on building materials ordered from distant provinces.

We can readily deduce from the Süleymaniye accounts that stone cut and blocked out in quarries and builders' yards conformed to regular specifications. This immediately raises the question how far Sinan's buildings were standardized overall. Özdural pertinently warns that units extracted from the present dimensions of his buildings will inevitably give unreliable results, but a preliminary survey by Neslihan Sönmez of Sinan's fenestration, based on measurements of height and breadth of the lower windows of seventeen of his mosques, has brought out some marked regularities. Notably, a fairly regular proportion of height to breadth suggests that the builders had a rule of thumb for scaling the windows up and down, from building to building or model to model. In the same building, for purely practical reasons, undue variation in window sizes and shapes seems to have been deliberately avoided, immensely simplifying the regular planning of both exterior façades and interior vistas.

It is more difficult to decide how much further standardization was taken: within the limits sketched out above there were many practical solutions and architects were not obliged to repeat themselves. An additional question that has received considerably less attention from Ottoman architectural historians is the possibility of modularity, the construction of buildings from units, either spatial (like the domed bays of an arcade, for example) or material (like the blocks of stone or timber that physically constitue them). Sinan's responsibilities as quantity surveyor, for the costing and supply of materials, imply at least a very limited scale of constituents, so that modularity goes hand in hand with standardization; but, except in a trivial sense, spatial modularity had built-in limits.

This was for two reasons: first, with any given set of construction materials statics imposes limits to the absolute size of the result, with consequent modifications to the constituent spatial blocks; and secondly, the reuse of architectural elements or spolia from other buildings must often have forced Sinan to take these as a given too. Evliyâ Çelebi's possibly fanciful story of Mehmed II's Court Architect, Âzâdlı Sinan's punishment for lopping the antique marble columns the Sultan provided for his mosque, Fâtih, by chopping off his hands shows how seriously an architect had to treat materials issued from the Imperial storehouse: their dimensions, rather than those he had decided on himself, had to come first. This was even more so with the massive granite columns, first of all from Alexandria and then from Baalbek, which Sinan incorporated into Süleymaniye, for the Ottomans do not seem to have had the tools to cut granite to size. Since they have an important structural role their height was an essential precondition of the total height of the mosque, which had to be built round them, so to say.

Finally, to the question of proportionality. It is odd in a way that this should have been given so much prominence in the history of European architecture, for it is only one of a series of factors that may affect our aesthetic response to a building and may often take second place to its absolute mass, for example, being used as a mere instrument to make a building appear larger than it actually is. Of course, it is possible that any building in a specific location, whatever its surroundings may be, may have an optimum size, making a scaled-down or scaled-up version less impressive, with the corollary that bad or ugly buildings might look better smaller.

Without explicit affirmations to the fact, it is virtually impossible to deduce an architect's intentions from his buildings. From, for example, Selimiye at Edirne we may conclude that Sinan built as large or as grand as he could, within the constraints of sight-lines, cost, or budget and the technical capacities of materials or the labour force: no doubt he could also have built on a miniature scale but he was not by inclination a miniaturist, unlike the builders of late fifteenth-century Mamluk Cairo. But to argue further that that these general aspirations were systematized in a theory of proportion is at best pointless, for we shall probably never know.

The treatises on proportionality of the Italian Renaissance theorists have no counterpart in Ottoman Turkey. As we have seen again and again, Sinan's training was essentially practical and although computer analysis might help us to determine whether his buildings, singly or as a whole, might enshrine certain regularities, the daunting task of photogrammetric recording has scarcely been begun. Moreover, as Wittkower has well said, in trying to prove that a system of proportion has been deliberately applied by an artist or architect it is easy to be misled into finding the ratios one wants, so one must look for unmistakable guidance by the artist himself. Ratios, in any case, may be seen to be observed while leaving the degree to which they may be interpreted unclear. Thus, although even to a superficial observer, it is apparent that proportion was an important factor in any of Sinan's buildings, in the absence of written documentation any systematic use of proportionality he might have made must remain a matter of speculation.

In the *Sûrnâme* of c.1582[1] there is admittedly a hint that Sinan's contemporaries attributed not merely practical but theoretical genius to him. Describing the parade of the architects and builders before Murad III, Intizâmî states that they were headed by their chief (*Üstad*)—who can only have been Sinan—at that date well over 90—bearing a six-stringed lute. He can scarcely have been playing it, even if he had played it when younger, and it must here be a symbolic attribute. The allusion would have been perfectly clear to the spectators. In the last book of Nizâmî's *Khamsa*, one of the favourite works of later Persian and Ottoman literature, Plato is credited with inventing an *organon*, not an organ but a six-stringed lute, and a special mode that so enchanted the animals which heard it that they fell into a slumber as if they were dead. The details here are inconsequential, but the six strings are a

---

[1]Topkapı Saray Library H.1344, fo. 192[b].

clear reminiscence of Pythagoras' generation of musical harmony from the ratios of the whole numbers one to six, which was adapted by Alberti from Vitruvius in his *De re aedificatoria* (c.1450). Though the Pythagorean and neo-Platonic strand in medieval Islam perpetuated the idea of proportion as the essence of beauty—without, however, recognizing a common proportionality between music and architecture as such—the lute Sinan bears here seems to imply a certain apprehension of current architectural theory in contemporary Italy. That said, it is fair to say that if, as is not impossible, a treatise by Alberti or one of his successors had come into Sinan's hands, he would not have made much of it.

8

Sinan's legacy

Sinan's achievement in bringing the Süleymaniye works to such a splendid conclusion was too valuable to be forgotten. They were the model for the mosque of Ahmed I on the Hippodrome under Mehmed Ağa and, even later, for Nuruosmaniye on the site of the Byzantine Forum of Constantine, for which on 14 Şevvâl 1161/7 October 1748 a three-dimensional model was ordered. Additional land was acquired to guarantee a spacious site. Workers were conscripted from all over Anatolia and the Greek islands. Marble columns (actually granite) were commandeered from Bergama, probably from the Roman temple of the Egyptian Divinities, and an official dispatched to measure them and arrange for their transport on sledges or low-loaders to the coast and thence by sea to Istanbul. The floor of the mosque was raised to a height decided by a committee including the Court Architect and the Inspector of Waterworks, the latter because the project demanded a new extension to the Kâğıthane system. As the digging of the foundations brought them below the water table the mosque was supported on a basement of great piers, with arches braced longitudinally and transversely by iron tie-rods. The works, as at Süleymaniye, took seven years and the mosque was inaugurated on 1 Rabî'ülevvel 1169/5 December 1755.

The dimensions of Sinan's buildings of the 1560s and 1570s increased spectacularly—though not their ornament, which Kuran argues, was largely confined to interiors, and to accents at that (the all-over tile decoration of the interior of the mosque of Rüstem Pasha is in many ways an aberration)—and, all in all, mark a steady progress to Selimiye at Edirne. Subsequently, progress gives way to a certain Mannerism: 'the dynamic quality and exaggerated plasticity of the 1580s is very different from the simple, clear-cut formal expression of the 1560s'. This suggests, perhaps, the diminution of Sinan's active role in this last period, and presages the clichés of even his most talented successors through the seventeenth century, by which time the classical style in Ottoman architecture had declined into unthinking orthodoxy. In some respects, this was perhaps the direct consequence of Sinan's contribution to the history of Ottoman architectural practice. For one thing (though it is scarcely his fault) his mastery of building forms tended to exhaust their possibilities and, as T. S. Eliot illuminatingly remarked of Milton's blank verse, deprived his successors of the opportunity of developing them any further. It goes without saying that Sinan was not the only inventor of Ottoman architecture as we know it, but had he not lived it, and Istanbul in particular, would have been far less splendid.

Though Imperial mosques at Edirne and in Istanbul had conventionally been domed from the Üç Şerefeli mosque at Edirne (841–51/1437–47), domes were lower and altogether less impressive, inside and out. And although the Imperial foundations of Mehmed II and Bayazid II at Edirne and in Istanbul were generously planned, the visual and spatial interrelation of their constituent buildings, which Sinan so brilliantly achieved at Süleymaniye, for example, was far less perspicuous and organized. Finally, although he built with conventional materials, the increasing standardization to which Palace registers and account books bear witness and which must be at least partly his achievement, enabled him and his successors to build on a scale that, without sacrificing structural stability in any way, would hitherto have been inconceivable.

Further Reading

It is difficult to write about Sinan without a knowledge of Turkish, Ottoman as well as the modern language. Fortunately, it is easier to read about him. The following books, all in English, give a more detailed picture of his achievements and the political, social, and economic climate in which he worked. Specific details may be found below under 'Other Primary and Secondary Sources', which for the adventurous reader may go some way towards supplying the deficiency of footnotes.

Crane, Howard, *Cafer Efendi, Risâle-i Mi'mâriyye* (Leiden, 1987).

Faroqhi, Suraiya, *Pilgrims and Sultans: The Hajj under the Ottomans, 1517–1683* (London, 1994).

Gibb, H. A. R., and Bowen, Harold, *Islamic Society in the Eighteenth Century*, in *Islamic Society and the West*. Part I (Oxford, London, 1950).

Goldthwaite, Richard, *The Building of Renaissance Florence: An Economic and Social History* (Baltimore, 1980).

Goodwin, Godfrey, *History of Ottoman Architecture* (London, 1971, etc.).

——, *Sinan, Ottoman Architecture and its Values Today* (London, 1993).

Inalcık, Halil, *The Ottoman Empire: The Classical Age 1300–1600* (London, 1973).

104 FURTHER READING

—, *A Social and Economic History of the Ottoman Empire*, vol. i 1300–1600 (Cambridge, 1994).

Kunt, I. Metin, *The Sultan's Servants: The Transformation of Ottoman Provincial Government, 1550–1650* (New York, 1983).

Kuran, Aptullah, *Sinan, The Grand Old Man of Ottoman Architecture* (Washington, DC and Istanbul, 1987).

Lybyer, H. A., *The Government of the Ottoman Empire in the Time of Süleyman the Magnificent* (Cambridge, Mass., 1913).

Mainstone, Rowland J., *Hagia Sophia: Architecture, Structure and Liturgy of Justinian's Great Church* (London, 1988).

Miller, Barnette, *The Palace School of Muhammad the Conqueror* (Cambridge, Mass., 1942).

Necipoğlu-Kafadar, Gülru, *Architecture, Ceremonial and Power: The Topkapı Palace in the Fifteenth and Sixteenth Centuries* (Cambridge, Mass, 1991).

Petruccioli, Attilio (ed.), 'Mimar Sinan: The Urban Vision', in *Environmental Design, The Journal of the Islamic Environmental Design Centre, Rome*, 5–6 (5th year)/ (Rome, 1987).

Riefstahl, R. M., *Turkish Architecture in Southwestern Anatolia* (Cambridge, Mass., 1931).

Rogers, J. M. and Ward, R. M., *Süleyman the Magnificent*, British Museum exhibition catalogue (London, 1988).

Sözen, Metin, *Sinan, Architect of Ages* (Istanbul, 1988).

OTHER PRIMARY AND SECONDARY SOURCES

Akalın, Şehabeddin, 'Mimar Dalgıç Ahmet Paşa', *Tarih Dergisi* 9 (1958), 71–80.

Akkuş, Mehmet, *Eyyûbî, Menâkib-ı Sultân Süleymân (Risâle-i Pâdişâh-nâme)* (Ankara, 1991).

Akkutay, Ülker, *Enderûn mektebi* (Ankara, 1984).

Akmandor, N., 'Koca Sinan'ın plâncılığı, eserleri ve mühendisliği', *Türkiye Mühendislik Haberleri* 157 (Apr. 1986), 4.

Aktaş-Yasa, Azize (ed.), *Uluslararası Mimar Sinan sempozyumu bildirileri (Ankara, 24–27 Ekim 1988)* (Ankara, 1996).

Anhegger, Robert, *Beiträge zur Geschichte des Bergbaus im*

osmanischen Reich: Europäische Türkei, 2 vols. (Istanbul and Zurich, 1943–4).

———, 'Istanbul su yollarının inşasına aid bir kaynak. Eyyûbî'nin Menâkib-i Sultan Süleyman'ı', *Tarih Dergisi* 1(1949), 119–38.

———, 'Beiträge zur frühosmanischen Baugeschichte', *Istanbuler Mitteilungen* 6 (1955), 89–108; 'Die Üç Şerefeli Camii in Edirne und die Ulu Cami in Manisa', *Istanbuler Mitteilungen* 8 (1958), 40–56; 'Moscheen in Saloniki und Serre: Zur Frage der T-plan Moscheen', *Istanbuler Mitteilungen* 17 (1967), 312–30.

Artan, Tülay, 'The Kadırga Palace: An Architectural Reconstruction', *Muqarnas* 10 (1993), 201–11.

———, 'The Kadırga Palace Shrouded by the Mists of Time', *Turcica* 26 (1994), 55–124.

Aslanapa, Oktay, 'Archivalien zur Geschichte der osmanischen Baukunst des 16. und 17. Jahrhunderts im Topkapı Serail Archiv zu Istanbul', *Anatolia* 3 (1958), 18–20.

Ateş, Ibrahim, *Mimar Sinan vakfı* (Istanbul, 1990).

——— *et al.* (eds.), VI. Vakıf haftası. *Türk vakıf medeniyeti çerçevesinde Mimar Sinan ve dönemi sempozyumu 5–8 Aralık 1988* (Istanbul, 1989).

Barkan, Ömer Lutfî, 'Edirne ve civarındaki bazı imâret tesislerinin yıllık muhasebe bilançoları', *Belgeler* 1/2 (Ankara, 1964), 235–377.

———, *Süleymaniye camii ve imareti inşaatı*, vols. i and ii (Ankara, 1972–9).

Béthier, P. A., *Nouvelles découvertes archéologiques faites à Constantinople* (Paris, 1867).

Bilge, Aygen, 'Mimar Sinan hakkında araştırmalar II', *Sanat Tarihi Yıllığı* V (Istanbul, 1973), 141–74.

Çeçen, Kâzım, *Süleymaniye suyolları* (Istanbul Teknik Üniversitesi İnşaat Fakültesi Matbaası, 1986).

———, 'Istanbul'un eski su tesisleri ve Kırkçeşme', in *Tarih boyunca Istanbul semineri 29 Mayıs-1 Haziran 1988. Bildiriler* (Istanbul, 1989), 197–209

———, *Istanbul'un vakıf sularından Halkalı suları* (Istanbul, 1991).

Celâlzâde Mustafa, *Geschichte Sultan Süleyman Kânûnîs von 1520 bis 1557*, oder *Tabakât ül-Memâlik ve Derecât ül-Mesâlik*, edited Petra Kappert (Wiesbaden, 1981).

Dagron, Gilbert, *Constantinople imaginaire* (Paris, 1984).

Denny, W., 'Sinan the Great as an Architectural Historian: The Kılıç Ali Pasha mosque in Istanbul', *Turcica* 15 (1983), 104–26.

Downes, Kerry, 'Vanbrugh, Sir John", *The Dictionary of Art* (London 1996).

Emecen, Feridun M., 'Manisa Muradiye camii inşâsına dair', *Tarih Enstitüsü Dergisi* 13 (1983–7) (Istanbul, 1987), 177–94.

Emerson, William and Robert L. Van Nice, 'Hagia Sophia and the first minaret erected after the conquest of Constantinople', *American Journal of Archaeology* 54 (1950), 28–40.

Erdoğan, Mustafa, 'Mimar Davud Ağa'nın hayatı ve eserleri', *Türkiyat Mecmuası* XII (1955), 179–204.

Eyice, Semavi, 'Sultaniye/Karapınar'a dair', *Tarih Dergisi* 20 (1965), 117–40.

Faroqhi, Suraiya, 'Trade and Traders in 1660s Iskenderun', in *Making a Living in the Ottoman Lands, 1480–1820* (Istanbul, 1995), 217–30.

Finkel, Caroline, and Barka, Aykut, 'The Sakarya River–Lake Sapanca–Izmit Bay Canal Project: A Reappraisal of the Historical Record in the Light of the Morphological Evidence', *Istanbuler Mitteilungen* 47 (1997), 429–42.

Gökyay, Orhan Şaik, 'Risale-i Mimariyye-i Mimar Mehmed Ağa— eserleri', *Ismail Hakkı Uzunçarşılı'ya Armağan* (Ankara, 1976), 113–215.

_____ (ed.), *Evliyâ Çelebi Seyâhatnâmesi 1* (Istanbul, 1996).

Goldthwaite, Richard, 'The Building of the Strozzi Palace: The Construction Industry in Medieval Florence', *Studies in Medieval and Renaissance History* (Lincoln, Neb., 1973), 99–194.

Gürlitt, Cornelius, *Die Baukunst Konstantinopels* (Berlin, 1912).

Harrison, Martin, *A Temple for Byzantium: The Discovery and Excavation of Anicia Juliana's Temple-Church in Istanbul* (London and Austin, Tex., 1989).

Hochhuth, Pia, *Die Moschee Nûruosmanîye in Istanbul: Beiträge zur Baugeschichte nach osmanischen Quellen* (Berlin, 1986).

Inalcık, Halil, 'Introduction to Ottoman metrology', *Turcica* 15 (1983), 311–48.

Jacob, Georg (ed.), *Deutsche Übersetzungen türkischer Urkunden, herausgegeben vom Orientalischen Seminar zu Kiel, Heft 4. Stambuler Urkunden, meist auf Bauwesen und Polizei bezüglich* (Kiel, 1920).

Kiel, Machiel, 'Remarks on Some Ottoman Turkish Aqueducts and Supply Systems in the Balkans—in Kavalla, Chalkis, Aleksinac, Levkas and Ferai/Ferecik', in *De Turcicis aliisque Rebus Commentarii Henry Hofman dedicati* (Utrecht 1992), 105–39.

Konyalı, Ibrahim Hakkı, *Mimar Koca Sinan* (Istanbul, 1948).

Kreiser, Klaus, *Edirne im 17. Jahrhundert nach Evliyâ Çelebî: Ein Beitrag zur Kenntnis der osmanischen Stadt* [=Islamkundliche Untersuchungen 33] (Freiburg-im-Breisgau, 1975).

———, 'Zur Kulturgeschichte der osmanischen Moschee', *Türkische Kunst und Kultur aus osmanischer Zeit*, exhibition catalogue, Museum für Kunsthandwerk (Frankfurt am Main, 1985) i, 75–86.

Kuban, Doğan, 'The Style of Sinan's Domed Structures', *Muqarnas* 4 (1987), 72–97.

Küçükkaya, Ayşe Gülçin, 'Mimarbaşı Sedefkâr Mehmed Ağa dönemi Edirne yapıları ve defterdar Ekmekçioğlu Ahmed Efendi', *Belleten* 55/212 (1991), 313–414.

Kuran, Aptullah, 'Mimar Sinan'ın ilk eserleri'/'Early works of the architect Sinan', *Belleten* 37 (1973), 154–8, 533–43, 545–56.

Kürkçüoğlu, K. E., *Süleymaniye vakfiyesi* (Istanbul, 1962).

Mango, Cyril, 'The conciliar edict of 1166', *Dumbarton Oaks Papers* 17 (1963), 317–30.

Martal, Abdullah, 'XVI. yüzyılda Osmanlı imparatorluğunda su-yolculuk', *Belleten* 52/205 (1988), 1586–1652.

Ménage, V. L., 'Some notes on the devşirme', *Bulletin SOAS* 29 (1966), 64–78.

Meriç, Rıfkı Melûl, *Mimar Sinan—Hayatı eseri I Mimar Sinan'ın hayatına, eserlerine dair metinler* (Ankara, 1965).

Mülayim, Selçuk, *Sinan ve çağı* (Istanbul, 1989).

Müller-Wiener, Wolfgang, *Bildlexikon zur Topographie Istanbuls: Byzantion—Konstantinopolis—Istanbul, bis zum Beginn des 17. Jahrhunderts* (Tübingen, 1977).

——, 'Das Kavak Sarayı—ein verlorenes Baudenkmal Istanbuls', *Istanbuler Mitteilungen* 37 (1988), 363–76.

Necipoğlu-Kafadar, Gülru, 'The Süleymaniye Complex in Istanbul: an Interpretation', *Muqarnas* 3 (1985), 92–117.

——, 'Plans and Models in Fifteenth and Sixteenth Century Ottoman Practice', *Journal of the Society of Architectural Historians* 45/3 (1986), 224–43.

——, 'The Life of an Imperial Monument: Hagia Sophia after Byzantium', in Robert Mark and Ahmet Ş. Çakmak (eds.) *Hagia Sophia, from the Age of Justinian to the Present* (Cambridge, 1992), 195–225.

——, 'Challenging the Past. Sinan and the Competitive Discourse of Early Modern Islamic Architecture', *Muqarnas* 10 (1993), 169–80.

Orhonlu, Cengiz, *Osmanlı Imparatorluğunda şehircilik ve ulaşım*, ed. S. Özbaran (Izmir, 1984).

Özdural, Alpay, 'Sinan's arşın: A Survey of Ottoman Architectural Metrology', *Muqarnas* 15 (1998), 101–15.

Öziş, Ünal and Arısoy, Yalçın, *Mimar Sinan'in suyolları* (Izmir, 1981).

Refik [Altınay], Ahmet, ed. Zeki Sönmez, *Türk mimarları* (Istanbul, 1977).

Rogers, J. M., 'The State and the Arts in Ottoman Turkey: The Stones of Süleymaniye', *International Journal of Middle East Studies* 14 (1982), 71–86.

——, 'The Furnishings and Decoration of Süleymaniye', *International Journal of Middle East Studies* 14 (1982), 283–313.

——, 'Sinan as Planner: Some Documentary Evidence', in Petruccioli (1987), 174–91.

——, 'Architectural Decoration in the Age of Sinan', in Aktaş-Yasa (1996), 285–96.

Saatçı, S., 'Tezkiretü'l-Bünyân'ın Topkapı Sarayı Revan kitaplığında yazma nüshası', *Topkapı Sarayı Müzesi, Yıllık* 4 (1990), 55–101.

Skilliter, Susan, *William Harborne and the Trade with Turkey, 1578–82* (Oxford, 1977).

Sönmez, Zeki, *Mimar Sinan ile ilgili tarihî yazmalar-belgeler* (Istanbul, 1988).

Sönmez, Neslihan, 'Mimar Sinan camilerinde alt sıra pencereleri boyutlandırma özellikleri', in Çiğdem Kafesçioğlu and Lucienne Thys-Şenocak (eds.), *Aptullah Kuran için yazılar/Essays in Honour of Aptullah Kuran*, Yapı-Kredi Kültür Yayınları (Istanbul, 1999), 287–309.

Turan, Şerafettin, 'Osmanlı teşkilâtında Hassa Mimarları', *Tarih Araştırmaları Dergisi* I (Ankara, 1963), 157–202.

——, 'Gli architetti imperiali (Hassa mimarları) nell'impero Ottomano', *Atti del Secondo Congresso Internazionale di Arte turca* (Naples, 1965), 259–63.

Ünsal, Behçet, 'Topkapı Sarayı arşivinde bulunan mimarî planlar üzerine', in *Türk San'atı Tarihi Araştırma ve İncelemeleri* I (1963), 168–97.

Uzunçarşılı, I. H., *Osmanlı devletinin saray teşkilatı* (repr. Ankara, 1984).

——, *Osmanlı devleti teşkilâtından kapukulu ocakları*, 2 vols. (repr. Ankara, 1984).

Wittkower, Rudolf, *Architectural Principles in the Age of Humanism* (revised edn., London, 1962).

Yenişehirlioğlu, Filiz, Emre Madran, and Ali Saim Ülgen *Mimar Sinan yapıları*, catalogue Türk Tarih Kurumu (Ankara, 1989).

Yerasimos, Stefanos, *La Fondation de Constantinople et de Sainte-Sophie dans les traditions turques* (Paris, 1990); trans. by Şirin Tekeli, *Kostantiniye ve Ayasofya efsaneleri* (Istanbul, 1993).

Glossary

Note. Already by 1550 the organization of the Ottoman Court was complex and the exact functions of its officials are often difficult to identify. Their titles, moreover, as at many courts, often refer to duties that had come to be superfluous or anachronistic. This sometimes makes it difficult to suggest an exact English equivalent. In the definitions below words shown in italics indicate terms that are defined elsewhere in this Glossary.

acem Persia, Persian. The Arabic *'ajam* appears originally to have been used as a general term for non-Arabs, sometimes with a certain derogatory implication. Hence Acemoiğlans, the untrained or unskilled Janissary private soldiers.

akçe A silver coin, the chief unit of account in the fifteenth- and sixteenth-century Ottoman empire. By the end of the reign of Mehmed II one Venetian ducat was roughly equivalent to about 45 akçe, but by around 1530–1550 the exchange rate had increased to about 55 akçe.

arabesque Interlacing foliate scrollwork, often symmetrical, with split palmettes or fat buds, known in Ottoman and modern Turkish as *rûmî*.

arpalık A kind of minor *timar*.

arşın The cubit, the standard of measurement in architecture. Around 1520 the builders' cubit (*bennâ arşını*) was equivalent to 72.1 cm, but by the later sixteenth century it had increased to 73.4 cm.

askerî The military or administrative class that performed various public functions as delegates of the Sultan and that accordingly was exempt from taxation.

Beglerbeg (modern Turkish *Beylerbeyi*) A military governor of a major province.

besmele (Arabic *basmala*) 'In the name of God, the Merciful, the Compassionate', the opening words of the Qur'an and customarily used as the opening of any text.

binâ emîni The Clerk of the Works appointed to oversee an Imperial building project, charged with the procurement of materials and dispensing the funds provided.

Bîrûn The outer section of the Sultan's household, including the Sultan's bodyguard, the *Hasekis* and the Master of the Horse (Imrahor) and other high administrative officials of the empire. Some were Janissary officers, but others were not *kapıkulları* at all.

bostancıs Initially, *devşirme* boys assigned to the Palace gardens, with a separate corps for the Palace at Edirne, also responsible for the maintenance and manning of the Sultan's barges and boats. They also included a group of distinguished officers or NCOs, the *Hassekis*, who served as the Sultan's own couriers and police. Their head, the Bostancı Başı, also had responsibility for policing the shores of the Bosphorus.

Çavuş Heralds, messengers, pursuivants, and later chamberlains in the suites of the Sultan or the Grand Vizier (*Dîvan-ı Hümâyûn*).

Celalis Miscellaneous disaffected elements rebelling against the central government from the sixteenth century onwards.

Complex, complex foundation A pious foundation consisting of different institutions of public welfare—*medrese*, *imaret*, hospital, *mekteb*, etc.—generally grouped together round a mosque.

Cuerda seca The use of waxed contours in the manufacture of polychrome glazed tiles to prevent the colours running in the firing.

defterdâr The Treasurer and Chief Accountant of the Ottoman empire, responsible for registering all income and expenditure.

devşirme An occasional levy of Christian children, mostly from Greece, Hungary and the Balkans, for training for high office in the Palace, the administration, and the military corps. They were the most famous, though not the most numerous, element of the Janissaries.

dirhem A silver coin, in the Arab provinces of the Ottoman empire equivalent to the *akçe*.

Divan (*Dîvân-ı Hümâyûn*) The Council of State presided over by the Grand Vizier that administered the Ottoman empire.

ebced The use of the letters of the Arabic alphabet with numerical values to form chronograms, where the total appropriately gives a particular date. For example, the Arabic word *kharâb* ('ruined') gives the date of Tamerlane's destruction of Damascus, 803/1400–1.

Enderûn. The inside service of the Sultan's Household, created under Mehmed II and substantially reformed under Selim I. An aristocracy of talent as well as privilege, from its members were recruited the Sultan's ministers and the highest military governors of the empire.

Fâtiha. The opening chapter of the Qur'an.

fetva (Arabic *fatwa*). An official decision on a point of Qur'anic law (*şeriat*, *sharî'a*) issued by the Şeyhülislâm (Arabic *Shaykh al-Islam*) or some other qualified official.

hadîs (Arabic *hadith*) A recorded tradition of the sayings and actions of the Prophet, in the light of which the text of the Qur'an may be interpreted.

hajj (or *hac*) Pilgrimage to the Holy Places of Islam, incumbent upon every Muslim at least once in a lifetime if he or she is able.

harem A ritual enclosure, primarily for the shrines at Makka and Madina (generally known as the Harameyn, the two Harams) and for the Dome of the Rock and the Aqsa Mosque at Jerusalem (al-Haram al-Sharif). Also used to indicate the domed prayer hall of a large courtyard mosque, or the women's quarters in a palace or private house.

Hâssa Mi'mars The Court Architect and his executive staff, charged with the execution of the Sultan's works.

Haseki Senior officers of the *Bostancıs* who served as the Sultan's police. Also Janissaries of distinction appointed to the Sultan's bodyguard.

hatâyî An Ottoman ornament of chinoiserie inspiration, especially based upon the Chinese cloud-scroll.

İçoğlans The cream of the *devşirme* boys who began their education at the Galata Saray or another of the pages' schools and who were then appointed to the staff of various Palace departments, such as the Pantry (*Kiler*) or the Treasury. The most important and influential were those in the Privy Chamber, who served as the Sultan's personal attendants. On passing out of the Palace service they could expect high military or administrative appointments.

ilmiye The professors and lecturers in the great Istanbul *medreses*, and their graduates, mostly judges, in the 'clerisy' of Istanbul and the Ottoman provinces.

imam The leader of prayers.

imaret Kitchen distributing food to the needy, by the reign of Süleyman the Magnificent an essential element of any Imperial pious foundation.

in'âmât defter The monthly Palace register of stipends and gratuities distributed to the royal ladies and their households, courtiers, and high officers.

Janissaries (Turkish *Yeniçeri*) The Ottoman crack troops, partly composed of boys recruited from the *devşirme*. Whereas under Mehmed II they probably numbered no more than eight to ten thousand, by 1600 they had swollen to between thirty-five and fifty thousand.

Khamsa The Quintet or Five Poems of the twelfth-century poet Nizami of Ganja in Azerbaijan is one of the most famous works of Persian literature. It was widely imitated by later poets in Persian, Uzbek (Chaghatay) and Ottoman, but the original remained a favourite work in Ottoman culture.

kadı (Arabic *qadi*) A judge, in the Ottoman empire often functioning as a provincial magistrate.

Kapıcı (literally 'Doorkeeper') The officers drawn from the *Bostancıs*, in the service of the Sultan or the *Dîvân-i Hümâyûn* charged with organizing Court ceremonial—feasts, parades, receptions. They also served as chamberlains and special messengers.

kapıkulları (literally 'slaves of the Porte') Primarily a product of the *devşirme*; members of a Janissary regiment; but, more generally, also anyone, either slave or free, employed in military, administrative or Palace service.

kaza Sub-district, administered by a *kadı*.

Kazasker (from Arabic *Qadı 'Askar* 'military judge') The highest posts in the Ottoman legal system, the Kazasker of Rumeli (the Ottoman empire in Europe) taking precedence over the Kazasker of Anatolia.

kul Soldier administrators, educated in the service of the state, who embodied the political and executive authority of the Sultan. Although some of these were juridically slaves, the term was often used to cover anyone legally in the Sultan's service.

medrese (Arabic *madrasa*) College, with a strong emphasis on Islamic law. From the time of Süleyman the Magnificent onwards the *medrese* system was highly centralized and its top graduates formed the *ilmiye*, who formed the most important element of the Ottoman bureaucracy.

mekteb A Qur'an school for orphans.

mihrab A niche in the wall of a mosque, indicating the direction of Makka, which the congregation faces to pray.

müezzin The giver of the call to prayer, attached to a mosque or other pious foundation.

Müfti The high legal official charged with giving opinions (*fetvas*) on problematic cases in the Muslim law. Under the Ottomans he had the rank of Şeyhülislâm (Arabic *Shaykh al-Islam*).

Müşârehorân (literally, 'those receiving monthly salaries') Groups of high officers and palace employees, primarily financial but also including entertainers, poets, musicians, buffoons, spies, and the Court Architect and his staff.

Müteferrika (literally, 'miscellaneous') An appropriately heterogeneous group of favoured courtiers in permanent attendance on the Sultan— heads of various army corps, members of princely families, musicians and, occasionally, craftsmen, though not, apparently, Sinan or his staff. They were rewarded variously by stipends or fiefs.

nahiye The smallest administrative unit in the Ottoman empire.

Nişancı The head of the Imperial Chancery, charged with drawing up documents of state in conformity with Ottoman law and with affixing the Sultan's monogram to them when they were issued or promulgated.

nisba An epithet, often relating to a person's lineage or provenance, and often used as a means of identifying him.

ocak Unit of military organization corresponding to a company or regiment (e.g. the Janissaries, or one of their smaller units) or even a division or corps (e.g. the Artillery). Their strengths naturally varied according to the circumstances.

qibla The direction of the Ka'ba (the sacred building at Makka), to which Muslims turn at prayer.

rahle Folding stand for a Qur'an or other precious book, usually of carved and inlaid wood and a standard piece of furniture for royal mausolea in Ottoman Turkey.

re'âyâ The merchants, craftsmen and peasants who constituted the production sector in the Ottoman economy and who accordingly paid taxes.

re'is Sea captain, often a corsair, in Ottoman service.

şadırvan Ornamental fountain or tank decorating the courtyard of a mosque or, as at Süleymaniye, serving as a central reservoir for the internal water supply. Though in later periods they were provided with taps and used for ablutions that was not their original purpose

Safavids Militant Shi'is of Sufi origin who gained power in Persia in 1501 and who were the Ottomans' principal enemies on the Eastern front.

sancak A military standard or banner; also a major fief or military governorate.

Şehremin One of four Palace commissioners (the others controlled the Imperial Kitchens, the Mint, and the Imperial Stables) in charge of provisions of all sorts for the Palace, including the Imperial storehouse of valuable building materials, and, in particular, the maintenance of the walls and water supply of Istanbul and its suburbs. Building in the city was controlled with the utmost rigour: to him were subordinated both the Court Architect (*Hâssa Mi'mar*) and the Inspector of Waterworks (*Suyolu Nâzırı*)

Şehzade The title of the Ottoman princes. The quarter Şehzadebaşı in Istanbul owes its name to the mosque built by Sinan in memory of Süleyman's favourite son, Şehzade Mehmed (d. 1543).

şeriat (Arabic *shari'a*) The holy law of Islam.

Şeyh (Arabic *shaykh*) A honorific term applied to heads of *medreses*, Sufi *zaviyes*, etc.

Şeyhülislâm (also known as *Müfti*) The head of the *ilmiye* in sixteenth-century Ottoman Turkey.

shari'a see şeriat

sipahis The Ottoman feudal cavalry, living on the taxes and dues collected from the peasantry on their land-holdings. In addition to providing campaign service they were charged with the maintenance of law and order. From the highest *sipahis* were generally drawn the provincial governors (Sancak Beg, *Beglerbeg*). They were later augmented by a paid cavalry (*Ulufecis*) recruited from the Janissaries. The large complement of *Içoğlans* among these gave them much greater prestige, which was emphasized by the splendour of their accoutrements.

Sultan In Ottoman usage, the title of the ruler of the empire. It was also accorded, as a courtesy title, to Ottoman princes. For princesses and royal ladies the title followed their names.

Suyolu Nâzırı Inspector of Waterworks. The official charged with the construction, maintenance, and repairs of the water supply of Istanbul and other Ottoman provincial cities. In the early decades of Sinan's career as Court Architect this came within his responsibilities, but from 1566 onwards it was made a separate post.

timar The grant, generally non-hereditary, of the tax revenues of an administrative district in payment for an office, on condition of campaign service with men and equipment. The principle is sufficiently similar to medieval European practice to justify calling it a fief, though in Europe such grants went not with the office but the individual. Fiefs with higher yields were termed *ze'âmet*.

vakf (plural *evkâf*; Arabic *waqf/awqaf*) Land, or other sources of revenue, immobilized in perpetuity for pious or charitable purposes, usually associated with foundations—a *medrese*, an *imaret*, a mosque, etc.— singly or in combination.

vakfiye (Arabic *waqfiyya*) The endowment deed of a pious foundation (*vakf*) giving the statutes and specifying in perpetuity the buildings endowed, with lists of staff on the foundation and their emoluments in money or kind.

Yayabaşı An infantry captain. The Yayas were an early Ottoman infantry, mostly rewarded with *timars*. By the sixteenth century they had come to be superseded by the Janissaries, and their role was rather that of a transport and pioneer corps, dragging guns, building roads, digging trenches and casting cannonballs.

ze'âmet see *timar*

zaviye Convent of dervishes or Sufis.

Zemberekçi The 82nd company or regiment (*ocak*) of the Janissaries, originally armed with crossbows and armour-piercing arrows. Their head, the Zemberekçibaşı, received 40 akçe a day. As the Janissaries came to be equipped with muskets, crossbows became obsolete, but the name persisted.

The Ottoman Sultans
824/1421–1026/1617

Murad II (first reign) 824–48/1421–44
Mehmed II (first reign) 848–50/1444–6
Murad II (second reign) 850–5/1446–51
Mehmed II (second reign) 855–86/1451–81
Bayazid II 886–918/1481–1512
Selim I Yavuz ('The Grim') 918–26/1512–20
Süleyman Kanunî ('The Lawgiver', more generally known in the West
    as 'The Magnificent') 926–74/1520–66
Selim II 974–82/1566–74
Murad III 982–1003/1574–95
Mehmed III 1003–12/1595–1603
Ahmed I 1012–26/1603–17

Chronological list of Sinan's major works

The following checklist is after A. Kuran, *Sinan, The Grand Old Man of Ottoman Architecture* (Washington, DC and Istanbul, 1987). Note that Sinan's responsibilities for repairs and maintenance of the Imperial palaces, the schools for pages and other public monuments of Istanbul, the shrines of the Harameyn, and the water supplies of Istanbul and Edirne were, we may assume, continuous and mostly, therefore, do not appear. Not all of his buildings bear a date, and even where they do, it is not always clear whether that commemorates the date works began, the date of inauguration, or the date the endowment deed was drawn up. To that extent, the chronological order given here is inevitably somewhat approximate.

935/1528–9 Svilengrad (Bulgaria), bridge of Çoban Mustafa Pasha.
946/1539–40 Istanbul (Avretpazarı), mosque, *medrese*, and *mekteb* of Süleyman's wife, Hürrem Sultan. The hospital was added, not necessarily by Sinan, c.1550.
948/1541–2 Istanbul (Beşiktaş), mausoleum of Süleyman's Admiral, Hayreddin Barbaros Pasha (Barbarossa).
950/1543–4 Istanbul (Şehzadebaşı), mausoleum of Şehzade Mehmed.
953/1546–7 Aleppo, mosque, and *medrese* of Hüsrev Pasha.
954/1547–8 Istanbul (Üsküdar), mosque, and *medrese* of Süleyman's daughter, Mihrimah Sultan.
955/1548–9 Istanbul (Şehzadebaşı), mosque, *medrese*, *mekteb*, *imaret*, and caravansaray of Şehzade.

958/1551 Istanbul (Silivrikapı), mosque and mausoleum of Hadim Ibrahim Pasha.

960/1552–3 Istanbul, Süleymaniye, First and Second medreses, Dârü'l-Tıbb (medical school).

962/1554–5 Istanbul, Süleymaniye, Dârü'l-Şifa (hospital), imaret.

962/1554–5 Damascus, mosque and imaret of Süleyman the Magnificent (al-Takiyya al-Sulaymaniyya).

964/1556–7 Istanbul (Ayasofya), double bath of Süleyman's wife, Hürrem Sultan.

964/1556–7 Istanbul, Süleymaniye, mosque, Dârü'l-Hadîs.

965/1557–8 Istanbul, Süleymaniye, mausoleum of Hürrem Sultan.

c.1557 Istanbul, the Kâğıthane waterworks

966/1558–9 Istanbul, Süleymaniye, Third and Fourth medreses.

post-1562 Istanbul (Tahtakale), mosque of Rüstem Pasha.

c.1564 Istanbul, the Kırkçeşme waterworks.

c.1565 Istanbul (Edirnekapı), mosque of Süleyman's daughter, Mihrimah Sultan. A medrese and hamam were added in 977/1569–70.

971/1563–4 Karapınar (Konya), imaret, caravansaray, and hamam.

974/1566–7 Damascus, medrese of Selim II.

974/1566–7 Istanbul (Süleymaniye), mausoleum of Süleyman the Magnificent

975/1567–8 Büyük Çekmece, mosque of Sokollu Mehmed Pasha, caravansaray, and bridges for Süleyman the Magnificent. Completed the following year.

979/1571–2 Istanbul (Kadırga), mosque, medrese, and tekke of Sokollu Mehmed Pasha.

981/1573–4 Istanbul (Kasımpaşa), mosque of Piyale Pasha.

c.1573–4 Major restorations and repairs to Hagia Sophia.

982/1574–5 Edirne, mosque of Selim II. The other elements of the complex were probably inaugurated in 980/1572–3.

982/1574–5 Payas (Yakacık), mosque, imaret, and caravansaray of Sokollu Mehmed Pasha.

985/1577–8 Istanbul (Ayasofya), mausoleum of Selim II.

985/1577–8 Vişegrad (Bosnia), bridge over the river Drina for Sokollu Mehmed Pasha.

c.1578–9 Istanbul (Toptaşı), mekteb, tekke, and imaret of the Valide, Nurbanu Sultan. The medrese is dated 987/1579–80 and the mosque, which evidently had to be rebuilt, 991/1583–4.

988/1580–1 Istanbul (Üsküdar), mosque, *medrese*, and mausoleum of Isfendiyaroğlu Şemsi Ahmed Pasha.

988/1580–1 Istanbul (Tophane), mosque, and mausoleum of Kılıç Ali Pasha. A *hamam* was added in 991/1583–4.

995/1586–7 Manisa, mosque, and *imaret* of Murad III (Muradiye).

Index

132 INDEX